# THE MINOR PR[...]
# Volume 3

### Ed Landry

**Obadiah**
**Haggai**
**Zechariah**
**Malachi**

**Uplifting Christian Books**
Nashville, Tennessee 2020

**The Minor Prophets - Volume 3**
#3 in the easy-to-understand Bible Commentary series on the Minor Prophets
Copyright © 2020 by Uplifting Christian Books

Published in Nashville, TN by Uplifting Christian Books
All rights reserved.

Printed in the Philippines by SAM Printing Press, Cebu City
Printed in the USA by Kindle Direct Publishing

Author - Ed Landry
Special thanks to our dedicated editorial team - Marcia P., Tom and Janet T., Herb M., Mitzi C., Ora Lee K., Dell W., Janet L., Lyndell M., Roy and Linda M., and Mike and Elaine F.
Book and cover design by Ed and Janet Landry.
Illustrations by Ed Landry.
Special thanks to The Bible Project for several small illustrations.
Additional Development team - The Thursday Group

ISBN-13: 978-0-9990931-5-3

Printed in the United States of America.

# Dedicated

To all the Pastors and Teachers of God's amazing Word. My hope is that these three volumes will inspire you to communicate the timeless messages found in the 12 minor prophets. The minor prophets are often neglected in pulpits and classrooms. My prayer is that these easy-to-read books will help bring them back to the people.

Ed Landry
Missionary, First Love International Ministries

# Some free recommended resources to help in your studies

### The Blue Letter Bible

This a free App (BLB) for your phones which has a wide spectrum of Bible study tools. To use on your computers and laptops, go to: **https://www.blueletterbible.org/**

### The Bible Project

A very creative group have produced these imaginative animations and charts of the books of the Bible. Each animation is around 5-6 minutes long and gives a great overview of the Word of God. They allow free downloads of their quality materials. **https://bibleproject.com/all-videos/**

### Precept Austin

A massive commentary and Bible resource website. The site contains word by word commentary of the entire Bible with some 20,000 resources. This site is for serious Bible students. One of the best organized and helpful sites on the internet. It will take a while to learn to navigate the site but worth the effort. **https://www.preceptaustin.org/**

### Got Questions

This online resource contains over 600,000 Bible questions and answers. Their leadership and staff represent some of the finest evangelical Bible colleges and seminaries in the USA. Comprehensive, yet concise.
**https://www.gotquestions.org/**

### Bible.Org

A large collection of commentaries and expostions arranged by topic, book, verse, words, etc. The site also has the NET Bible (2nd edition) with its 58,000+ notes, Greek, Hebrew, texts linked to Strongs numbers. It allows you to search all the translations of the Bible to find your favorite verses. The commentary section uses the works of hundreds of top theolgians and evangelical authors. Find it at:
**https://bible.org/**

### Bible Hub

A huge collecton of word studies, commentaries, Bible versions. Type in a verse and then choose what you want and you will have more resources than you can imagine. Like any web site, it will take a little time to understand it and take advantage of its power.
**https://biblehub.com/**

# OBADIAH

## The coming destruction of Edom

"But the house of Esau will be as stubble.
And they will set them on fire and consume them,
So that there will be no survivor of the house of Esau,
For the LORD has spoken."

Obadiah 18

# Introduction
## THE STORY OF EDOM, ISRAEL'S GREATEST ENEMY

**"A man's pride will bring him low, but a humble spirit will obtain honor" (Proverbs 29:23).**

An introduction to the book of Obadiah requires more than the usual who, what, where, and when. The most important question that needs to be answered is "why." Why was this book written? It is a prophecy about the coming destruction of the Edomites, the descendants of Esau, Jacob's brother. Why would God want to exterminate a race of people? Before we answer that question, let's first meet Obadiah.

## THE BOOK OF OBADIAH

With one chapter and only 21 verses, Obadiah is the shortest book in the Old Testament. We can't date when Obadiah was written, but scholars believe all evidence leads to two possible time periods, 853-841 B.C. or 605-586 B.C. These two dates are based on how certain events mentioned in Obadiah are interpreted, concerning invasions of Jerusalem. Without going into the details, we will have to be satisfied to accept that a definite time of writing is not possible. Good scholars disagree and so they believe different dates. Obadiah gives us no personal information in his short book. I have included Obadiah in the Persian reign, around the time of the 70-year captivity, which is 605-586 B.C. Most likely, the description in Obadiah 1:11-14 of the Edomites mocking, looting and taking advantage of the Israelites, following a major defeat, is describing the fall of Jerusalem in 586 B.C.

That would make him current, or just after Jeremiah in the land of Judah during the captivity. Obadiah's name means "servant of Yahweh." The book is a proclamation of judgment on the enemies of Israel. It would have been a great encouragement to the nation of Israel to know God had not forgotten them and was bringing judgment on the people that tormented and mocked them and the name of God.

**To understand Obadiah we need to understand Edom.**

## WHERE WAS EDOM?

Edom was the land occupied by the line of Esau, Jacob's brother. It was larger than Judah, the southern kingdom, extending all the way to the Gulf of Aqaba in the west. The land was south of Israel. Today the land is part of Jordan and Saudi Arabia. Today, Edom no longer exists.

## THE PRIDEFUL EDOMITES

Edom is a mountainous region south of the Dead Sea. The sheer cliffs are filled with caves where the Edomites lived and fought invaders. They became arrogant in their safe havens high above the ravines below. They felt invincible and were proud to live where eagles nested and arrows could not reach them. It is important to know this to understand the book.

One of the most famous of these sites today is the ancient city of Petra, which was once occupied by the Edomites. Their location not only protected them but allowed them to control the ancient trade routes that went from Arabia in the south to Damascus in the north. Here are three photos of the region. The first is the famous treasury building carved out of the hillside in Petra.

### Petra, the Ancient City - The Inhabitants

Who inhabited Petra, the Ancient City? It is believed that the earliest inhabitants of this mysterious area were the Horites (Genesis 14:6). Evidence indicates that Petra's first occupants were cave-dwellers. Esau, the brother of Jacob, settled in the area south of the Dead Sea. His descendants, the Edomites, eventually replaced the Horites (Genesis 36). The mountains of Edom still abound with caves, temples, and houses cut in the side of the mountain surrounding Petra. The Edomites built almost impregnable fortresses in the canyons and gorges of these mountains. The magnificent ruins at Petra attest to the greatness which Edom once knew. (All about Archeology)

This second photo is a sample of the numerous caves where the Edomites lived and resisted invading armies.

The third photo (below) is the Corinthian Tomb.

The background of Obadiah is the story of Esau, Jacob's brother, and Edom, the land where he settled. When we understand the history of Edom, we learn why God inspired the prophet, Obadiah, to pronounce such a devastating judgment against the people of the land. Other prophets, as well, pronounced judgment on Edom.

# A very important brief history

### THE BIRTH OF ESAU

"When her days to be delivered were fulfilled, behold, there were twins in her womb. Now the first came forth red, all over like a hairy garment; and they named him Esau. Afterward, his brother came forth with his hand holding on to Esau's heel, so his name was called Jacob; and Isaac was sixty years old when she gave birth to them." (Genesis 25:24-26)

### ESAU DESPISED HIS BIRTHRIGHT AND IS CALLED EDOM

"When Jacob had cooked stew, Esau came in from the field and he was famished; 30 and Esau said to Jacob, 'Please let me have a swallow of that red stuff there, for I am famished.' Therefore, his name was called Edom. But Jacob said, 'First sell me your birthright.' Esau said, 'Behold, I am about to die; so of what use then is the birthright to me?' And Jacob said, 'First swear to me'; so he swore to him, and sold his birthright to Jacob. Then Jacob gave Esau bread and lentil stew; and he ate and drank, and rose and went on his way. Thus, Esau despised his birthright." (Genesis 25:29-34)

### WHEN ESAU DESPISED HIS BIRTHRIGHT HE TURNED HIS BACK ON GOD, FOREVER.

"That there be no immoral or godless person like Esau, who sold his own birthright for a single meal. For you know that even afterwards, when he desired to inherit the blessing, he was rejected, for he found no place for repentance, though he sought for it with tears."
(Hebrews 12:16-17)

## ESAU MARRIED INTO A PAGAN NATION, THE NORTHERN HITTITES

"When Esau was forty years old he married Judith the daughter of Beeri the Hittite, and Basemath the daughter of Elon the Hittite; and they brought grief to Isaac and Rebekah." (Genesis 26:34,35)

"They (*the Hittites*) are repeatedly mentioned throughout the Hebrew Tanakh (also known as the Christian Old Testament) as the adversaries of the Israelites and their God. According to Genesis 10, they were the descendants of Heth, son of Canaan, who was the son of Ham, born of Noah" (Genesis 10: 1-6).
*(Ancient History Encyclopedia)*

## ESAU (EDOM) WAS POLLUTED WITH FALSE RELIGION AND REBELLION AGAINST GOD

"Puduhepa, a queen and priestess of the Hittite religion prayed: 'Sun-Goddess of Arinna, my lady, you are the queen of all lands! In the land of Hatti, you have assumed the name of Sun-Goddess of Arinna, but in respect to the land which you made of cedars, you have assumed the name Hebat.'" (13th century B.C.E inscription)

## THE LAND OF EDOM (WHERE ESAU SETTLED) BECAME ISRAEL'S GREATEST ENEMY

"The oracle of the word of the Lord to Israel through Malachi. 'I have loved you,' says the Lord. But you say, 'How have You loved us?' 'Was not Esau Jacob's brother?' declares the Lord. 'Yet I have loved Jacob; but I have hated Esau, and I have made his mountains a desolation and appointed his inheritance for the jackals of the wilderness.' Though Edom says, 'We have been beaten down, but we will return and build up the ruins'; thus says the Lord of hosts, 'They may build, but I will tear down; and men will call them the wicked territory, and the people toward whom the Lord is indignant forever.'" (Malachi 1:2-4)

### ESAU'S GRANDSON, AMALEK WAS THE WORST OF THEM ALL. GOD COMMANDED HIS PEOPLE TO WIPE THE NAME "AMALEK" OFF THE EARTH.

"Therefore it shall come about when the Lord your God has given you rest from all your surrounding enemies, in the land which the Lord your God gives you as an inheritance to possess, you shall blot out the memory of Amalek from under heaven; you must not forget." (Deuteronomy 25:19)

### LATER, GOD TOLD KING SAUL THAT THE TIME HAD COME TO ERADICATE AMALEK

"Then Samuel said to Saul, 'The Lord sent me to anoint you as king over His people, over Israel; now therefore, listen to the words of the Lord.' Thus says the Lord of hosts, 'I will punish Amalek for what he did to Israel, how he set himself against him on the way while he was coming up from Egypt. Now go and strike Amalek and utterly destroy all that he has, and do not spare him; but put to death both man and woman, child and infant, ox and sheep, camel and donkey.'" (1 Samuel 15:1-3)

# Summary of Esau and Edom

To fully understand the importance and influence of Edom, you would need to read through much of the Old Testament and some ancient history as well. Since we don't have space to do that here, let me give a short summary of that history.

God chose Abraham to be the father of a nation to bring His Son into the world. Abraham had Isaac who had Jacob and Esau. Esau turned his back on God and sold his birthright to his brother Jacob. Jacob replaced Esau and received the blessings of the firstborn son of Isaac. Jacob's name was changed to "*Israel*." Israel became the chosen nation to bring Jesus, the Messiah, into the world. Esau became the father of a different people, one that hated Israel and wanted them destroyed. The Edomites (which includes the

Amalekites) became Israel's greatest enemy. Hatred for Israel is part of the DNA of Edom. According to the covenant God made to Abraham, anyone that cursed Israel would be cursed by God. If there was a book written called "Cursed by God," Edom would be on the cover.

It is this curse and the final destruction of Edom that Obadiah addressed. It is the same judgment Ezekiel warned was coming:

> **"Because of what Edom did against the house of Judah by taking vengeance, and has greatly offended by avenging itself on them, therefore thus says the Lord GOD: 'I will also stretch out My hand against Edom, cut off man and beast from it, and make it desolate from Teman; Dedan shall fall by the sword. I will lay My vengeance on Edom by the hand of My people Israel, that they may do in Edom according to My anger and according to My fury; and they shall know My vengeance,' says the Lord GOD."**
>
> (Ezekiel 25:12-14)

# Obadiah Commentary
## The day of judgment is coming upon Edom (1-14)

### THE ARROGANT PEOPLE OF EDOM WILL BE BROUGHT LOW (1-4)

¹ The vision of Obadiah.
Thus says the Lord GOD CONCERNING EDOM—
WE HAVE HEARD A REPORT FROM THE LORD,
And an envoy has been sent among the nations *saying*,
"Arise and let us go against her for battle"—
² "Behold, I will make you small among the nations;
You are greatly despised.

$^3$ "The arrogance of your heart has deceived you,
You who live in the clefts of the rock,
In the loftiness of your dwelling place,
Who say in your heart,
'Who will bring me down to earth?'
$^4$ "Though you build high like the eagle,
Though you set your nest among the stars,
From there I will bring you down," declares the LORD.

## EDOM'S FATAL FLAW

It was April 10, 1912. Spring had begun, banners flew, bands played, and children were laughing. What was once considered the greatest ocean liner in the world left on its maiden voyage from England to cross the Atlantic Ocean on its way to New York City. The ship was so large, so magnificent, so invincible, that the captain of the Titanic, Edward John Smith, proclaimed *"Even God Himself couldn't sink this ship."* Four days later the great ship was resting on the bottom of the Atlantic Ocean along with 1,500 passengers who couldn't fit into the few lifeboats on board. The Titanic only had a few because they wouldn't be needed, the ship couldn't sink. Captain Smith also drowned on that night the "unsinkable" ship went down. The entire event was a rebuke against the arrogance of man.

Edom was the Titanic of the nations. It was doomed from the start. The day Esau despised his birthright to be the promised heir of the line of Israel, was the worst decision anyone has ever made. His entire family line was cursed from that day forward.

The Titanic had fatal flaws built-in that were ignored. It was great and powerful, so what could happen? Likewise, Edom was flawed but ignored its sins and became proud. Many nations feared them. They built their homes in the mountains, carved out by hand. They lived high on the cliffs with the eagles, nobody could hurt them. Even God Himself could not defeat the Edomites, so they thought.

> **"The arrogance of your heart has deceived you,**
> **You who live in the clefts of the rock,**
> **In the loftiness of your dwelling place,**
> **Who say in your heart,**
> **'Who will bring me down to earth?'"** (3)

Who will bring them down to earth? Only the God of Heaven and earth that said: *"Pride comes before destruction, and an arrogant spirit before a fall."* (Proverbs 16:18, Holman Christian Standard Bible) From several passages in Jeremiah and the historical books of the Bible, we can see that Edom trusted in several things that could not save them. They were known for their philosophy and wisdom. The Edomites had made several alliances with other nations. Also, their homes were carved in stone and high above the narrow entrances to their canyon fortress. This was a secure and indestructible military advantage. The only thing they didn't have was God.

## THE FALL OF EDOM WILL BE DEVASTATING (5-9)

[5] "If thieves came to you,
If robbers by night—
O how you will be ruined!—
Would they not steal *only* until they had enough?
If grape gatherers came to you,
Would they not leave *some* gleanings?
[6] "O how Esau will be ransacked,
*And* his hidden treasures searched out!
[7] "All the men allied with you

Will send you forth to the border,
And the men at peace with you
Will deceive you and overpower you.
*They who eat* your bread
Will set an ambush for you.
(There is no understanding in him.)
[8] "Will I not on that day," declares the LORD,
"Destroy wise men from Edom
And understanding from the mountain of Esau?
[9] "Then your mighty men will be dismayed, O Teman,
So that everyone may be cut off from the mountain of Esau
by slaughter.

## THE DESTRUCTION WILL BE COMPLETE (5, 6)

If a robber broke in and stole your goods, he would leave when he took what he wanted to steal. Normally he would not burn the house down and remove all evidence that a house ever stood on that site. If someone broke into your garden and took some grapes to eat, they would leave when they were filled. They wouldn't uproot all the trees in the vineyard and destroy all the other crops already packed up to go to market. They would eat their fill and leave.

When God brings His judgment on Edom it will be so severe the people would wish robbers had come upon them. At least something would remain. It would be a total ransacking, nothing overlooked, even things hidden in secret places would be found and destroyed.

### NO FRIENDS OR ALLIES WILL SAVE YOU (7)

All the alliances you formed to guarantee your security will fail you and abandon you on the day of your destruction. They will even be the ones who defeat you. Your allies once ate at your table and now they will steal your bread to feed themselves and destroy your ovens and tables. Your destruction will come when you least expect it. It will be an ambush. The only one that can be trusted in life is God and you turned your back on Him.

## YOUR "WISE" LEADERS WILL FAIL YOU (8, 9)

Edom had its philosophers and prided itself on having accumulated wisdom and understanding. Obadiah warns, they will not be there when you need them. They will not have a solution or answer. Your mighty men will also fail. They will be confused and confounded not knowing what to do. The slaughter will be great. Nothing you have trusted will deliver you. The reason for this extreme judgment is given in the next verse. It was the violence Esau caused to his brother, Jacob. Over the years the Edomites and Amalekites attacked and killed the Israelites. This began when Esau rejected God and Jacob followed God.

If Edom wondered what sinful acts caused them to be judged, they only needed to read the next five verses.

## GOD LISTS THE CHARGES AGAINST THE LAND OF ESAU (10-14)

10 "Because of violence to your brother Jacob,
You will be covered *with* shame,
And you will be cut off forever.
11 "On the day that you stood aloof,
On the day that strangers carried off his wealth,
And foreigners entered his gate
And cast lots for Jerusalem—
You too were as one of them.
12 "Do not gloat over your brother's day,
The day of his misfortune.
And do not rejoice over the sons of Judah

In the day of their destruction;
Yes, do not boast
In the day of *their* distress.
<sup>13</sup> "Do not enter the gate of My people
In the day of their disaster.
Yes, you, do not gloat over their calamity
In the day of their disaster.
And do not loot their wealth
In the day of their disaster.
<sup>14</sup> "Do not stand at the fork of the road
To cut down their fugitives;
And do not imprison their survivors
In the day of their distress.

## LET ME SUMMARIZE THE CHARGES AGAINST THE PEOPLE OF EDOM.

- Edom had organized violent attacks against Israel. (10)
- Edom ignored the pleas of Israel in the time of their distress. (11)
- In arrogance, Edom didn't just watch foreign nations plunder Israel, but were guilty participants in the wicked acts. (11)
- When Judah was being destroyed by an enemy army, Edom mocked Israel. They rejoiced over the loss of Jerusalem and even took credit for the victory. (12)
- After the destruction of Jerusalem, Edom arrogantly entered the gates of the city and "gloated" over the disaster. Instead of mourning loss of life and property, Edom was wickedly satisfied with the pain, suffering, and losses of Judah. Remember this is Esau laughing and mocking the tragedy that has befallen his brother, Jacob. It is a depraved sin, not just a lack of compassion. (10, 13)
- Then Edom looted the wealth of the land. They kicked Judah when they were down. They mocked them and they

stole everything from them while they were helpless. (13)

- When some of the Israelites escaped the invasion, the Edomites lay in wait on the road to ambush the survivors. The ones they didn't kill, they imprisoned. (14)
- The nation of Edom proved to be a heartless, evil people whose one purpose in life was to destroy the people of God. By the way, when you meet Haman in the book of Esther, watch him do everything he could to have all the Jewish people exterminated. Remember, he is a descendant of Esau, an Amalakite.

These verses sound like a prosecuting attorney laying out the evidence of a crime before the judge to get a conviction. The evidence is overwhelming and compelling. Edom is guilty of vicious crimes against humanity and Israel in particular. The only verdict that can come is the death penalty for such treacherous hatred. They hated God and hated their neighbors. The entire broken Law of God screams the verdict, "Guilty as charged!"

How many times in our lives have we cried out to God for justice when we have seen people get away with sin? We always need to remember this passage. God is always keeping the records and one day the books will be opened and . ... well, we will let God finish the sentence:

> "Then I saw a great white throne and Him who sat upon it, from whose presence earth and heaven fled away, and no place was found for them. And I saw the dead, the great and the small, standing before the throne, and books were opened; and another book was opened, which is the book of life; and the dead were judged from the things which were written in the books, according to their deeds. And the sea gave up the dead which were in it, and death and Hades gave up the dead which were in them; and they were judged, every one of them according to their deeds. Then death and Hades were thrown into the lake of

**fire. This is the second death, the lake of fire. And if any-
one's name was not found written in the book of life, he
was thrown into the lake of fire."**
(Revelation 20:11-15)

Jeremiah captured the emotions of the captives who were in
Babylon in Psalm 137. He lamented over the treatment of Israel
by two nations. The first is the mocking by Babylon who asked
them to sing some of the songs of Israel for their entertainment.
They refused and even hung their instruments on the trees.
The second lament was against Edom who rejoiced when the
city of Jerusalem fell while they chanted, "Raze it, raze it to its
very foundation", or in other words, "Burn it to the ground!" The
emotions ran so deeply that the Jewish people cried out for
vengeance against their tormentors. They said they would
praise the one who would one day destroy the family line of
those vicious people, including the children. Try to picture the
deep emotions as you read Jeremiah's words:

> **"By the rivers of Babylon,**
> **There we sat down and wept,**
> **When we remembered Zion.**
> **Upon the willows in the midst of it**
> **We hung our harps.**
> **For there our captors demanded of us songs,**
> **And our tormentors mirth, saying,**
> **'Sing us one of the songs of Zion.'**
> **How can we sing the LORD'S SONG**
> **In a foreign land?**
> **If I forget you, O Jerusalem,**
> **May my right hand forget her skill.**
> **May my tongue cling to the roof of my mouth**
> **If I do not remember you,**
> **If I do not exalt Jerusalem**
> **Above my chief joy.**
> **Remember, O LORD, AGAINST THE SONS OF EDOM**
> **The day of Jerusalem,**

Who said, 'Raze it, raze it
To its very foundation.'
O daughter of Babylon, you devastated one,
How blessed will be the one who repays you
With the recompense with which you have repaid us.
How blessed will be the one who seizes and dashes your
little ones against the rock."
(Psalm 137:1-8)

The day would come when the cries of the people of God would
be answered. Babylon fell and the royal family line was
exterminated. Edom was wiped off the earth and today Israel is
back in their homeland while the other two empires are gone.
God had warned, *"be sure your sin will find you out."*
(Numbers 32:23). It did.

# The day of the Lord is coming (15-21)

## THE DAY OF THE LORD WILL BRING BLESSING FOR THE SONS OF JACOB AND DESTRUCTION TO THE SONS OF ESAU. (15-18)

[15] "For the day of the LORD DRAWS NEAR ON ALL THE
NATIONS.
As you have done, it will be done to you.
Your dealings will return on your own head.
[16] "Because just as you drank on My holy mountain,
All the nations will drink continually.
They will drink and swallow
And become as if they had never existed.
[17] "But on Mount Zion there will be those who escape,
And it will be holy.
And the house of Jacob will possess their possessions.
[18] "Then the house of Jacob will be a fire

And the house of Joseph a flame;
But the house of Esau *will be* as stubble.
And they will set them on fire and consume them,
So that there will be no survivor of the house of Esau,"
For the LORD HAS SPOKEN.

This portion begins with a warning to the sons of Esau, "*As you have done, it will be done to you. Your dealings will return on your own head,*" (15). The Golden Rule Jesus gave is normally viewed as a positive promise that we should treat people the way we would like to be treated. It has a negative element as well. If we treat people poorly aren't we saying, this is how I want to be treated? Even Eastern religions recognize this principle when they talk about karma. Scientists see this principle when they say any force has an equal and opposite reaction. The Proverbs say it this way:

> **"He who digs a pit will fall into it, And he who rolls a stone, it will come back on him."** (Proverbs 26:27)

What God expected of man was not complicated. The prophet Micah was clear.

> **"He has told you, O man, what is good;**
> **And what does the LORD REQUIRE OF YOU**
> **But to do justice, to love kindness,**
> **And to walk humbly with your God?"**
> (Micah 6:8)

## THREE THINGS WERE EXPECTED AND EDOM FAILED AT ALL THREE.

- **To treat people justly.** Edom acted treacherously, even ambushing Israel, taking advantage of their weak condition. That is the opposite of treating people in a just or right fashion.

- **To act kindly to others.** Edom ambushed the citizens of Jerusalem when they fled the destruction of the city. They murdered the Israelites in the same way they attacked the elderly ones during the Exodus from Egypt when they lagged behind the multitude.

> **"Remember what Amalek did to you along the way when you came out from Egypt, how he met you along the way and attacked among you all the stragglers at your rear when you were faint and weary; and he did not fear God. Therefore it shall come about when the Lord your God has given you rest from all your surrounding enemies, in the land which the Lord your God gives you as an inheritance to possess, you shall blot out the memory of Amalek from under heaven; you must not forget."**
> (Deuteronomy 25:17-19)

- **To walk humbly before God.** We have seen that the pride or arrogance of the sons of Esau, the Edomites and Amalekites, was repulsive to God. God always resists the proud and gives grace to the humble. They stubbornly refused to bless Israel. God had told Abraham that He would not bless any people that did that. (Genesis 12:2, 3)

The next promise we see in these verses is that God will use Israel to punish Edom. God's children will be the fire and Edom will be the burned up firewood. In other words, God will use Israel to execute His wrath against His enemies.

Edom drank on "*God's holy mountain*" along with the attacking nations. The very place set apart for God, the temple, the priests and sacrifices were made a mockery by Edom. They mocked and feasted at the holiest of places that God set apart to show mankind the way of salvation by faith. It was a slap in the face of God Himself (16-18). Edom had turned from God and had no right to enter the Holy Place and disgrace it. It was almost a preview of the Abomination of Desolation Jesus warned about which will occur in the last days when the Temple will be defiled by the Antichrist.

The final promise at the end of this passage (18) is *"there will be no survivor of the house of Esau, for the Lord has spoken."* God is never mocked, whatever a man sows, that is what he will reap (Galatians 6:7). Today, you will not find an Edomite.

## THE LAND WILL BE DELIVERED TO THE SONS OF JACOB (19-21)

<sup>19</sup> Then *those of* the Negev will possess the mountain of Esau,
And *those of* the Shephelah the Philistine *plain*;
Also, possess the territory of Ephraim and the territory of Samaria,
And Benjamin *will possess* Gilead.
<sup>20</sup> And the exiles of this host of the sons of Israel,
Who are *among* the Canaanites as far as Zarephath,
And the exiles of Jerusalem who are in Sepharad
Will possess the cities of the Negev.
<sup>21</sup> The deliverers will ascend Mount Zion
To judge the mountain of Esau,
And the kingdom will be the Lord's.

This final section of Obadiah ends with the words, *"And the kingdom will be the Lord's."* The children of the promise will be back in their land and God will reign over them. Edom will be no more and the Lord will be the rightful King over the land. Israel will possess the land that once belonged to Edom. This is a future prophecy, most likely the Millennial reign of Christ. This is an ultimate fulfillment of what we are instructed to pray in the Lord's prayer, *"Your Kingdom come, Your will be done on earth as it is in heaven."* (Matthew 6:10)

## SEVERAL THINGS ARE PROMISED IN THESE FINAL VERSES

- The great Day of the Lord is coming, a time of judgment and reigning.
- Judgment will be against the Gentile nations, who have been enemies of God, as it was against Edom.
- The Jewish people will ultimately triumph over their enemies.
- Israel will be returned and possess her God-appointed land and even the land of her enemies.
- God's Kingdom will come to Earth.

**This is the same time spoken of by the prophet Amos:**

**"I will plant them in their land, and no longer shall they be pulled up from the land I have given them. Says the Lord your God."** (Amos 9:15)

Verse 21 mentions *"deliverers"* (some versions translate the word as "saviors.") In these last days, Edom will not have anyone to deliver them. The people of God will and these deliverers will become judges against Edom.

There are differing views as to who these deliverers might be, and it is probable we may not know the answer yet. Many times, the prophets themselves did not fully understand the very words they were inspired to record. The following passage from Daniel is one example:

**"As for me, I heard but could not understand; so I said, 'My lord, what will be the outcome of these events?' He said, 'Go your way, Daniel, for these words are concealed and sealed up until the end time. Many will be purged, purified and refined, but the wicked will act wickedly; and none of the wicked will understand, but those who have insight will understand.'"** (Daniel 12:8-10)

Here is one perspective on the identity of the deliverers from a theological commentator:

> "These deliverers may be resurrected saints who return with Jesus. Since they are said *to judge*, we could infer that these are among those who reign with Jesus at the establishment of His kingdom at the beginning of the millennium.
>
> > 'And I saw thrones, and they sat on them, and judgment was committed to them . . .'" (Revelation 20:4)
>
> "Or perhaps these 'deliverers' are heroic Jewish individuals who, like the judges of Israel's past, are raised up by God as part of the overthrow of Edom associated with the events leading to the Second Coming. A similar idea may be expressed by Zechariah when he describes leaders among Judah who are enabled by God to do great exploits in association with the events of the Second Coming." (Tony Garland, Th.M., Th.D.)

## LESSONS WE LEARN FROM OUR JOURNEY WITH OBADIAH

**God will completely defeat His enemies.**

We may at times feel like the wicked are escaping their judgment, but they aren't. Psalm 73 is a helpful picture of this. The Psalmist struggles with the prosperity of the wicked. Why do the godly struggle so much when the sinners seem to get away with sin and even become wealthy because of their sin? Why do they have a life of ease when believers don't? How is this fair? God shows him the following great truth that God sees and judges everything. Nothing escapes His notice or justice:

> "When I pondered to understand this,
> It was troublesome in my sight
> Until I came into the sanctuary of God;

Then I perceived their end.
Surely You set them in slippery places;
You cast them down to destruction.
How they are destroyed in a moment!
They are utterly swept away by sudden terrors!"
(Psalm 73:16-19)

**When we oppose the people of God we oppose God Himself.**
Edom learned this lesson the hard way. In the book of Acts, Gamaliel gave a similar warning to the Jewish ruling council:

> "So in the present case, I say to you, stay away from these men and let them alone, for if this plan or action is of men, it will be overthrown; but if it is of God, you will not be able to overthrow them; or else you may even be found fighting against God." (Acts 5:38, 39)

**There are no secret sins with God.**
I once listened to a military soldier answering questions about going to war against terrorists in the Middle East. He was asked a question about what was one thing that surprised him in battle. The soldiers today from developed countries have infrared devices that allow them to see in the dark. Many of their campaigns are fought at night. This soldier answered the question saying, *"The most surprising thing to me is that the enemy we fight actually believes we can't see them after dark. They think they are hiding!"* Because Edom was not quickly judged, they developed false confidence that they were safe. God's timing is up to Him but there will be an exposure of all sin and a day of reckoning. Our sins are never hidden from God.

> "for it is disgraceful even to speak of the things which are done by them in secret. But all things become visible when they are exposed by the light." (Ephesians 5:12, 13)

"'Can a man hide himself in hiding places so I do not see him?' declares the LORD 'Do I not fill the heavens and the earth?' declares the LORD." (Jeremiah 23:24)

## The sinner has no place to hide.

The Edomites built their homes in the most inaccessible places, caves high on rugged canyon walls. They boasted that nobody could bring them down or overthrow them.

"Where can I go from Your Spirit?
Or where can I flee from Your presence?
If I ascend to heaven, You are there;
If I make my bed in Sheol, behold, You are there."
(Psalm 139:7, 8)

"But do you suppose this, O man, when you pass judgment on those who practice such things and do the same yourself, that you will escape the judgment of God?"
 (Romans 2:3)

"Then I saw a great white throne and Him who sat upon it, from whose presence earth and heaven fled away, and no place was found for them. And I saw the dead, the great and the small, standing before the throne, and books were opened; and another book was opened, which is the book of life; and the dead were judged from the things which were written in the books, according to their deeds."
(Revelation 20:11, 12)

# HAGGAI

## Challenging the people to complete the Temple reconstruction

"This people says, 'The time has not come, even the time for the house of the LORD to be rebuilt.'"

Haggai 1:2

# Introduction

Imagine you owned a manufacturing company. A recent fire has destroyed your facilities and you decide to rebuild the factory. You hire a contractor to do the project. You decide it is a good time to take a long-deserved vacation and since the factory is not operational yet and you have someone taking care of everything. This is a good time to get your mind off the tragedy. With all the building material purchased and workers hired, you leave for your holiday.

Three weeks later you return expecting to see some progress. You are shocked to find that not only has all work stopped at the building site but the contractor and workers have used the construction materials to do room additions on their own personal homes. How would you feel?

This describes what was happening in Haggai's time. Jerusalem and the temple were destroyed by the Babylonians and the people were taken captive and held hostage for 70 years. Then they were permitted to come home and 50,000 returned along with a godly governor, Zerubbabel, and a High Priest, Joshua. It was time to get the Temple rebuilt after it had been burned to the ground. However, it didn't all happen right away.

> "It was almost twenty years after the decree of Cyrus when the prophet Haggai was called to bring the word of God to the people of Jerusalem in 520 B.C. Following the return from Babylon, the people had begun well, completing the rebuilding of the altar in 537 B.C. and preparing the temple foundation in 536 B.C. Opposition and other problems, however, had caused discouragement to set in, and work on the temple had ceased for over fifteen years. The people became occupied with their own personal concerns and the temple remained in ruins. Haggai called on the people to get their priorities straight."
> (Ligonier Ministries)

Why had the people stopped rebuilding the temple? The book of Ezra gives us some history about this event:

> **"Then the people of the land discouraged the people of Judah, and frightened them from building, and hired counselors against them to frustrate their counsel all the days of Cyrus king of Persia, even until the reign of Darius king of Persia."** (Ezra 4:4, 5)

> **"So the work on the Temple of God in Jerusalem had stopped, and it remained at a standstill until the second year of the reign of King Darius of Persia."** (Ezra 4:24)

Instead of rebuilding the temple, the people began doing room additions and using temple materials to panel their homes. God gave Haggai the prophet an assignment and a message to get the people back on track and get the job done.

> **"When the prophets, Haggai the prophet and Zechariah the son of Iddo, prophesied to the Jews who were in Judah and Jerusalem in the name of the God of Israel, who was over them, then Zerubbabel the son of Shealtiel and Jeshua the son of Jozadak arose and began to rebuild the house of God which is in Jerusalem; and the prophets of God were with them supporting them."** (Ezra 5:1 ,2)

They needed to stop their selfish attitude and put God first. God used Haggai to expose their sin and get them to start working again. It was the year 520 B.C. Haggai delivered four messages from God to his people. One thing unusual about his messages is that the Jewish people actually listened and obeyed, at least for a while. Haggai may be the second smallest book in the Old Testament but its message is as relevant today as it was in his day. Haggai's name means "Festival of Yahweh." He had been dedicated to God at birth.

The work and will of God should always be our top priority. God will not bless anyone who follows his own way and ignores the

Word of the Lord. Israel definitely learned this lesson the hard way. The captivity itself was a judgment for not heeding the Word of God. The numerous, extensive warnings in Deuteronomy 28 are very clear.

> **"Thou shalt beget sons and daughters, but thou shalt not enjoy them; for they shall go into captivity."**
> (Deuteronomy 28:41)

The chart below shows that the history of Israel is a series of cycles of falling into apostasy and idolatry and then repenting and then doing it all over again.

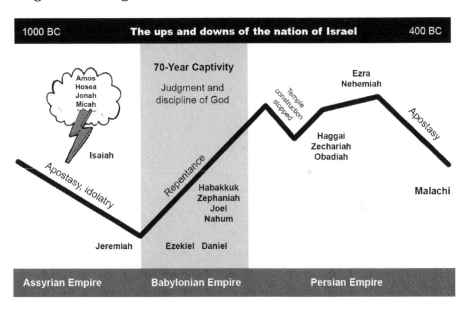

# Haggai 1
## The first of 4 messages Haggai delivers to his people

## STOP PUTTING YOUR OWN PERSONAL DESIRES AHEAD OF GOD'S PLAN (1:1-3)

[1] In the second year of Darius the king, on the first day of the sixth month, the word of the Lord came by the prophet Haggai to Zerubbabel the son of Shealtiel, governor of Judah, and to Joshua the son of Jehozadak, the high priest, saying, [2] "Thus says the Lord of hosts, 'This people says, "The time has not come, even the time for the house of the Lord to be rebuilt."'" [3] Then the word of the Lord came by Haggai the prophet, saying, [4] "Is it time for you yourselves to dwell in your paneled houses while this house lies desolate?"

It is sad to see the words "this people" instead of "My people" when Israel is addressed by the prophet. There is a sense of disgust over their sin of neglecting the Temple reconstruction. When Solomon first built the original Temple, he built it before his own house. Now the people want to build their fancy houses before the Temple. God has been pushed to the back of the line.

Remember the young man who once told Jesus that he wanted to follow Him but he wanted to bury his father first?

> **"And He said to another, 'Follow Me.' But he said, 'Lord, permit me first to go and bury my father.' But He said to him, 'Allow the dead to bury their own dead; but as for you, go and proclaim everywhere the kingdom of God.'"**
> (Luke 9:59, 60)

On the surface, this may sound like a heartless response to that person but something important needs to be understood. The man's father was not dead. What he was saying was "Jesus, I want to follow you, but I have other things I want to do first. I have things I have planned to do with my life. One day my father will die and then I will follow you." Jesus' answer was clear that nothing should be more important than the Kingdom of God and doing His will.

This is what was happening in Haggai's time. The people had returned from a 70-year captivity in Babylon. Now they were back home. They had plans to get their lives going again. God wanted the temple rebuilt and the people were saying, "OK, we will build it but not yet. We want to build our own houses first. Then we will do what you want us to do." To make matters worse, they built their homes with materials that were to be used on the Temple.

Why was that Temple so important to God? The Temple was a picture of the cross of Christ in the Old Testament. It pointed the way to salvation through faith. It was the message of hope for a lost world and God is not willing that any should perish, but all come to repentance (2 Peter 3:9). The people's refusal to rebuild theTemple was telling God that His plan of salvation was not as important, as it was for them to live in fancy houses ("*paneled homes*" was a description of excess luxury at that time).

## *NOTE TO PASTORS AND TEACHERS:
### *A very relevant message for our people today.*

It is a dangerous thing to neglect the work of God to attain wealth, status or comfort. The things that do not satisfy cannot compare with the joy of peace with God and the blessings He brings to those who follow Him completely. A practical application for us today would be the Great Commission. Many claim to believe that God has called us to preach the Gospel to all people yet they don't pray, give or go to make it happen. Are we any different from the selfish Jewish exiles in the days of Haggai who pursued personal comfort and status over obedience to God? We need to see the bigger picture of a life that honors God rather than the passing pleasures of sin. If Haggai lived today would he have a different message for us or the same one?

---

## WHAT HAPPENS WHEN WE NEGLECT THE WORD AND WORK OF GOD (1:4-11)

[5] Now therefore, thus says the LORD of hosts, "Consider your ways! [6] You have sown much, but harvest little; *you* eat, but *there is* not *enough* to be satisfied; *you* drink, but *there is* not *enough* to become drunk; *you* put on clothing, but no one is warm *enough*; and he who earns, earns wages *to put* into a purse with holes."

The phrase "consider your ways" has been described in the Hebrew language to mean "you have put your heart on the wrong road or path. You need to really think about this. Is this the path you want to travel down?"

Work on the temple began when the exiles returned but then the work stopped for 14 years. It was time for a prophet of God to step up and that man was Haggai. Haggai told the people to look around and pay attention to what had been happening in their lives. They worked every day but not for the things God told them to do. Because of that, the blessings of God had been withheld.

Their cupboards were empty, their bank accounts were empty, and their lives were empty. Jesus would later tell His audiences the same thing when He said to seek, first of all, the Kingdom of God and His righteousness, because if they would do that then God would provide their needs (Matthew 6:33). The Exiles in the day of Haggai became well aware of what happens to a person who does not put the things of God first. Emptiness, and more emptiness was the result. Haggai pled with the people to just look around and see what was happening. The same thing happened earlier according to the Psalmist:

**"And he gave them their request; but sent leanness into their soul."** (Psalm 106:15)

## THE FUTILITY OF RESISTING GOD (1:7-11)

<sup>7</sup> Thus says the LORD of hosts, "Consider your ways! <sup>8</sup> Go up to the mountains, bring wood and rebuild the temple, that I may be pleased with it and be glorified," says the LORD. <sup>9</sup> *"You* look for much, but behold, *it comes* to little; when you bring *it* home, I blow it *away*. Why?" declares the LORD of hosts, "Because of My house which *lies* desolate, while each of you runs to his own house. <sup>10</sup> Therefore, because of you the sky has withheld its dew and the earth has withheld its produce. <sup>11</sup> I called for a drought on the land, on the mountains, on the grain, on the new wine, on the oil, on what the ground produces, on men, on cattle, and on all the labor of your hands."

Someone once joked, "Cheer up, things could be worse. So we cheered up and, yes, things got worse!" For Israel, things went from bad to worse. If you are going to pick a fight, it is best not to pick God to fight against. The Lord told the people to go to the mountains and get wood for building materials. They already used the materials set apart for the temple construction for personal gain. Here is a list of what God did because of the selfishness and sins of the people:

- The dreams and hope of the people were broken.
- The anger of God raged against them like a mighty storm in their faces.
- The rain was stopped, not even dew formed on the ground. Their lives became as dry as desert land.
- Plants, fruits, and vegetables withered in the face of the great drought that scourged the land.
- The drought and famine were so widespread it affected, not just the ground, but the cattle and ultimately the

37

people themselves. Life became a burden, fruitless and empty.

These things should not have been a surprise since God warned them in the time of Moses before they entered the land. He promised to them that troubling times were coming for any who disobeyed Him.

> **"Beware that your hearts are not deceived, and that you do not turn away and serve other gods and worship them. Or the anger of the Lord will be kindled against you, and He will shut up the heavens so that there will be no rain and the ground will not yield its fruit; and you will perish quickly from the good land which the Lord is giving you."** (Deuteronomy 11:16,17)

Remember, we are just as capable of ignoring the eternal Kingdom of God for the temporary delights of this world, just as Israel did. The people of Israel thought their hearts' delight could be solved by worldly pleasures like a comfortable house. Jesus said He would provide the things we need if we seek his righteousness first. Nothing fulfills the human heart like God.

> **"What else does this craving, and this helplessness, proclaim but that there was once in man a true happiness, of which all that now remains is emptiness? He tries in vain to fill this with everything around him, though none can help. This infinite abyss can be filled only by God himself."** (Blaise Pascal)

## THE PEOPLE REPENT AND RETURN TO WORK (1:12-15)

¹² Then Zerubbabel the son of Shealtiel, and Joshua the son of Jehozadak, the high priest, with all the remnant of the people, obeyed the voice of the LORD their God and the words of Haggai the prophet, as the LORD their God had sent him. And the people showed reverence for the LORD.

<sup>13</sup> Then Haggai, the messenger of the LORD, spoke by the commission of the LORD to the people saying, "'I am with you,' declares the LORD." <sup>14</sup> So the LORD stirred up the spirit of Zerubbabel the son of Shealtiel, governor of Judah, and the spirit of Joshua the son of Jehozadak, the high priest, and the spirit of all the remnant of the people; and they came and worked on the house of the LORD of hosts, their God, <sup>15</sup> on the twenty-fourth day of the sixth month in the second year of Darius the king.

Remember the chart that showed the nation had its ups and downs. They would follow God, then turn from God, then repent and follow God. This part of the story is one of the good parts. Israel determined to follow God again putting His will first. God's response was "*I am with you.*" No matter how often we fail, He is with us if we just turn to Him.

All the people *"showed reverence for the Lord."* From the leadership to the everyday worker, true worship returned to the land and remained throughout the entire building of the Temple. It was a work of God and not just a determination of man. The spirit of God stirred the spirits of the people. It was real repentance and revival.

> **"So the LORD stirred up the spirit of Zerubbabel the son of Shealtiel, governor of Judah, and the spirit of Joshua the son of Jehozadak, the high priest, and the spirit of all the remnant of the people; and they came and worked on the house of the LORD of hosts, their God"** (1:14)

It was a great time of encouragement and refreshing from God. As the Temple began to take shape, there was a problem. It became obvious to those who had seen the original Solomon's Temple before it was destroyed, that the new Temple could not match the former glory of Solomon's Temple. It was time for another message from God. We see that in chapter 2.

# Haggai 2
## Three more messages for God's neglectful people

### HAGGAI'S MESSAGE 2 (2:1-9)

¹ On the twenty-first of the seventh month, the word of the Lord came by Haggai the prophet saying, ² "Speak now to Zerubbabel the son of Shealtiel, governor of Judah, and to Joshua the son of Jehozadak, the high priest, and to the remnant of the people saying, ³ 'Who is left among you who saw this temple in its former glory? And how do you see it now? Does it not seem to you like nothing in comparison? ⁴ But now take courage, Zerubbabel,' declares the Lord, 'take courage also, Joshua son of Jehozadak, the high priest, and all you people of the land take courage,' declares the Lord, 'and work; for I am with you,' declares the Lord of hosts. ⁵ 'As for the promise which I made you when you came out of Egypt, My Spirit is abiding in your midst; do not fear!' ⁶ For thus says the Lord of hosts, 'Once more in a little while, I am going to shake the heavens and the earth, the sea also and the dry land. ⁷ I will shake all the nations, and they will come with the wealth of all nations, and I will fill this house with glory,' says the Lord of hosts. ⁸ 'The silver is Mine and the gold is Mine,' declares the Lord of hosts. ⁹ 'The latter glory of this house will be greater than the former,' says the Lord of hosts, 'and in this place I will give peace,' declares the Lord of hosts."

### DON'T FEAR THE DAY BECAUSE GOD HAS GREAT PLANS FOR YOU! (2:1-9)

Have you ever started out to do something with a great vision?

But it didn't turn out like you were planning. It was going to be beautiful but now it has become ordinary. The joy seemed to disappear. The enthusiasm changed. What was the use in continuing since it was not happening the way you had pictured it? That is what happened to Israel. Discouragement had set in. The new Temple was not as beautiful as the first Temple. Nothing about the new one matched the glory of the original. They didn't want to continue. What they needed was a new vision, God's vision. God knows things we don't. It was time to see what He sees. It wasn't just about the time then, but there was a greater purpose in the future. God is the only One who could explain it all.

There were some who had seen the original Temple and they discouraged the people with the news.

> **"Yet many of the priests and Levites and heads of fathers' households, the old men who had seen the first temple, wept with a loud voice when the foundation of this house was laid before their eyes, while many shouted aloud for joy, so that the people could not distinguish the sound of the shout of joy from the sound of the weeping of the people, for the people shouted with a loud shout, and the sound was heard far away."** (Ezra 3:12-13)

God then told all the people to take courage because even though the new Temple was not the same in glory as the original, it was still a part of the plan of God. After all, it was a temple with the worship services, the sacrifices, the feasts and all that a temple is designed to facilitate. Nothing had changed. Outward appearance had nothing to do with function. That is a good lesson we can learn today. He reminded them that the God who delivered the Hebrew children was the same God that was saying the new temple was also part of His plan.

God then told them that the nation of Israel had once shaken the world but a day is coming when He will shake all nations, the earth, the dry land, and the sea. The glory of God will cover the earth and the glory of the temple then will be greater than ever in human history. This is the only passage from the book of Haggai that is quoted in the New Testament in Hebrews 12:26. It is referring to the end times.

> **"And His voice shook the earth then, but now He has promised, saying, 'Yet once more I will shake not only the earth, but also the heaven.'"** *(Hebrews 12:26)*

The final chapter of the story has not yet been written but it is coming. God challenged them to see the reconstructed temple through the eyes of faith. It was all part of God's plan. His message was "Don't look back and compare, but look forward with faith." When we live making comparisons, we will always find someone better or something nicer. This message from Haggai reminds us today that nothing compares to God. His glory is greater than any man-made thing. His wisdom and knowledge far exceed the wisest on the earth. His power is far beyond the mightiest of people or leaders. We need to stop looking around and look up. Do what He says. Believe that His way is best.

God reminds the people that everything is His, gold, silver, the temple, the entire earth, **everything**. He lacks nothing.

---

# *NOTE TO PASTORS AND TEACHERS:
### *A very relevant message for our people today..*
## THE DANGER OF COMPARING OURSELVES WITH OTHERS

A person who compares himself with another is not wise. We need to believe the promises of God, not the fears of man. We need to fully use the gifts God has given us instead of wishing we had other gifts. Only those things done for Christ will last. We can only do this when our focus is on the Eternal God and not the temporal world. It is only when we set aside our small dreams for the greater plan of God that the "Desire of all nations" (Christ) will be taken to the nations that need to hear. *"For the mind set on the flesh is death, but the mind set on the Spirit is life and peace."* (Romans 8:6)

## HAGGAI'S MESSAGE 3 (2:10-19)

[10] On the twenty-fourth of the ninth month, in the second year of Darius, the word of the Lord came to Haggai the prophet, saying, [11] "Thus says the Lord of hosts, 'Ask now the priests for a ruling: [12] If a man carries holy meat in the fold of his garment, and touches bread with this fold, or cooked food, wine, oil, or any other food, will it become holy?'" And the priests answered, "No." [13] Then Haggai said, "If one who is unclean from a corpse touches any of these, will the latter become unclean?" And the priests answered, "It will become unclean." [14] Then Haggai said, "'So is this people. And so is this nation before Me,' declares the Lord, 'and so is every work of their hands; and what they offer there is unclean.

## THE SIN IN OUR LIVES MAKES EVERYTHING WE TOUCH UNCLEAN! (2:10-14)

The people of Haggai's day understood the Old Testament Law. They just did not understand what it meant. They went through mandatory religious exercises yet their lives were like the famine in the land without fruit. Haggai in this section is given an assignment by God to ask some questions to the priests. Then God uses the answers to make an application to the nation as a whole. The verdict is that the nation was unclean

43

and everything they offered to God was unclean.

There were two points to the questions.

- The first is that if you are carrying something holy, or set apart for God, and if that item touches another thing, it does not make that thing holy. Holiness cannot be ransmitted from one thing or person to another.
- The second point is that corruption is different. Something infected or rotten can make another thing or person corrupted, rotten, or sinful. Sin can transmit or infect, unlike holiness.

A person who is sick can make a healthy person sick but the sick person cannot become healthy by touching a healthy person.

What was the purpose of this exercise? God told Haggai that it is a picture of the nation. They had become sick. Sins of disobedience had led to selfish behavior. They abandoned the will of God to pursue personal pleasure. That corruption, like a disease, infected the entire nation like a plague. The deception was that they somehow felt that they could be called healthy because they were the children of Abraham. They were part of the chosen people. They reasoned that they had the Law and priests and therefore the favor of God. In other words, just being around healthy people like the priests and heritage of their nation was enough to make them healthy. Therefore, God's proclamation about them was *"every work of their hands; and what they offer there is unclean."* (2:14)

Here is how one commentator described the situation:

> **"Since their exile to Babylon, the people of Israel focused on *getting back to the Promised Land.* In and of itself this was not a bad focus, yet it led to the thinking that once they made it back to the Promised Land everything else would be good. Haggai reminded them that their presence in the Promised Land doesn't make everything they do**

holy. If the priorities of our heart are wrong, nothing we
do is really holy to God." (Guzik, Blue Letter Bible)

Another way to think of the scene in Haggai's time is that the
burned-out temple was like a dead body lying in the street. It
was spreading decay and corrupting the nation. The people
mistakenly thought just being around theTemple made them
healthy. It was the same thing that Jeremiah warned the people
about before the destruction of the first temple.

> "Do not trust in deceptive words, saying, 'This is the
> temple of the Lord, the temple of the Lord, the temple of
> the Lord.'
>
> Then I will make to cease from the cities of Judah and
> from the streets of Jerusalem the voice of joy and the voice
> of gladness, the voice of the bridegroom and the voice of
> the bride; for the land will become a ruin."
>
> (Jeremiah 7:4, 34)

---

# *NOTE TO PASTORS AND TEACHERS:
## *A very relevant message for our people today.*
## CAN GOOD WORKS MAKE A PERSON RIGHT WITH GOD?

The Jews trusted in their heritage, family line, priests, the Law,
circumcision, religious feasts, sacrifices, and the temple. Some who
call themselves Christians cling to their church membership,
having a Bible, going regularly to services, doing good deeds,
having a certain pastor, being respected, etc. As good as these
things may be, they are not what make us a Christian. If that is all
we are clinging to, they can actually prevent us from becoming a
Christian. They can become distractions from salvation by faith

alone. Good works must come from a real relationship with Christ, they don't make us right with God. John 1:12 is a key verse.

---

## BLESSINGS TO COME (2:15-19)

<sup>15</sup> But now, do consider from this day onward: before one stone was placed on another in the temple of the Lord, <sup>16</sup> from that time when one came to a grain heap of twenty measures, there would be only ten; and when one came to the wine vat to draw fifty measures, there would be only twenty. <sup>17</sup> I smote you and every work of your hands with blasting wind, mildew and hail; yet you did not come back to Me,' declares the Lord. <sup>18</sup> 'Do consider from this day onward, from the twenty-fourth day of the ninth month; from the day when the temple of the Lord was founded, consider: <sup>19</sup> Is the seed still in the barn? Even including the vine, the fig tree, the pomegranate and the olive tree, it has not borne fruit. Yet from this day on I will bless you.'"

"Mark this day on your calendar." This is in essence what God was telling the people. Up to this point, the blessing of God has been withheld from them because of disobedience. God reminded them again why the calamities of the past have come upon them. At the same time, He gave them a glimmer of hope that days of blessing are yet up ahead. The people needed to consider these things. Did they want to continue in calamity or trust God with their whole hearts? Then they would experience the blessings of God. These blessings were promised from the time the first temple was completed and they still are alive but the people needed to believe God to see them come to pass.

These verses were like a review of a history lesson. It was a lesson, unfortunately, that the people did not learn. When we do not learn from our mistakes, we will travel that same path again until we change our behavior.

> **"Those who fail to learn from history are condemned to repeat it."** (Winston Churchill)

The good news is that we can change. That is what God was telling Israel. In the past when they came to the grain storehouse to get 20 measures, they could only get 10 because of the famine in the land. God had sent storms, hail, and mildew against the work of the farmer's hands. The land had produced little but God is saying those days are ending. The blessing of God is back if the people will come back to God.

# Haggai's final message for the nation (2:20-23)

## GOD IS GOING TO SHAKE THINGS UP! (2:20-23)

[20] Then the word of the Lord came a second time to Haggai on the twenty-fourth day of the month, saying, [21] "Speak to Zerubbabel governor of Judah, saying, 'I am going to shake the heavens and the earth. [22] I will overthrow the thrones of kingdoms and destroy the power of the kingdoms of the nations; and I will overthrow the chariots and their riders, and the horses and their riders will go down, everyone by the sword of another.' [23] 'On that day,' declares the Lord of hosts, 'I will take you, Zerubbabel, son of Shealtiel, My servant,' declares the Lord, 'and I will make you like a signet ring, for I have chosen you,'" declares the Lord of hosts.

The people were given a great opportunity, not just for blessings for their day, but to be a part of a much greater story for their people. God was lifting the veil, so to speak, and letting them peek behind the scenes at what is coming in the distant future. They could be participants or remain as spectators, but God is planning a spectacular finish to history. He is going to shake the nations, the heavens, and the earth. God will defeat every world leader and demolish all strongholds. The armies of the enemy nations will be overthrown in a mighty victory. The only historical event that matches this description will be the ending of the last great war and the return of Christ to set up His millennial Kingdom.

At that time, He will honor those who have been faithful.

> **"If we endure, we will also reign with Him;**
> **If we deny Him, He also will deny us."** (2 Timothy 2:12)

This New Testament passage in 2 Timothy gives us the choice. We can be faithful and endure trials for God and He will give us a place in reigning with Him or we can deny His calling in our lives and He will deny us that privilege.

He particularly focuses on Zerubbabel. The signet ring signifies royal authority. Although we can't be certain what all this means, it seems to say Zerubbabel is given a place of prominence in that day of the Lord when He shakes the nations and sets up His Kingdom on earth. It could also be, as some commentators believe, that the honor given to Zerbabbel is that he is part of the prominent line of the lineage of Christ.

> **"It was easy for the returning exiles to feel insignificant**
> **in the world as if they were just pawns or spectators. God**
> **wanted them to know that though they were small in the**
> **eyes of the superpowers of the world, they were servants**
> **of the God of all power. They are on the winning side."**
> (Guzik)

# *NOTE TO PASTORS AND TEACHERS:

*A very relevant message for our people today.*
## CARPE DEUM – SEIZE THE DAY!

When great opportunities from God are given, there are no good reasons to hesitate. Doors do not always stay open long. Delayed opportunities are often lost opportunities.

> **"Today if you hear His voice,**
> **Do not harden your hearts as when they provoked Me,**
> **As in the day of trial in the wilderness,**
> **Where your fathers tried Me by testing Me,**
> **And saw My works for forty years.**
> **Therefore I was angry with this generation,**
> **And said, 'They always go astray in their heart,**
> **And they did not know My ways';**
> **As I swore in My wrath,**
> **'They shall not enter My rest.'"**
>
> (Hebrews 3:7-11)

> **"We must work the works of Him who sent Me as long as it is day; night is coming when no one can work."** (John 9:4)

This thought really sums up the book of Haggai. The people of Israel had been through a well-deserved discipline by God for ignoring His commands. God, in grace, brought them back to their land and gave them the opportunity to build again and get a fresh start. They returned to their old pattern of ignoring God and built nice homes for themselves to enjoy the comforts of their land. God did not honor that decision and brought a great drought on the land and the people themselves. God then gave them yet another chance to get right with Him and promised to bless them abundantly if they would just follow Him. However, that offer was not to last forever.

What will we do with the opportunities God has given? We know His commands. Will we serve God or ourselves? Will we seize the day, the moment while it is day and we can work before the night comes? The message of Haggai is for us today. What will we do?

Years ago, I was talking to a friend of mine. He was a very strong Christian who was quite elderly at that time. He reached into his pocket and pulled out a few coins. He told me his life was like those coins, mostly spent now, with only a few coins left. Then he said, "I want to be very careful how I spend them!"

Isn't that the same message of Haggai? If we use our time and resource to enrich ourselves, we are just making ourselves poorer since God will not bless us.

> **"Consider your ways! You have sown much, but harvest little; you eat, but there is not enough to be satisfied; you drink, but there is not enough to become drunk; you put on clothing, but no one is warm enough; and he who earns, earns wages to put into a purse with holes."**
> (Haggai 1:6)

# ZECHARIAH

**Completing the Temple, rebuilding the priesthood, proclaiming judgment against Israel's enemies, and prophesying about the coming Messiah.**

This is the word of the Lord unto Zerubbabel, saying Not by might, nor by power, but by My spirit, saith the Lord of hosts

Zechariah 4:6

# Introduction
## The promise of a new beginning and a glorious future of hope

Are you ready for visions, dreams, burdens, oracles, proclamations, and lamentations? Zechariah is a wild excursion that literally takes us from the beginning of Israel's journey to the end of time. It chronicles the victories, the failures, the judgments, the struggles, the sins, the blessings and the future hope of Israel, the apple of God's eye. Zechariah was clearly a man of great compassion and brutal honesty. He was a man of God with a message from God to a people who had a tendency to forget their God. Reading Zechariah is a breathtaking pilgrimage into the heart of God Himself. There is no simple way to adequately describe the book. It's vistas, stories, poetry and hopes reach far beyond simple words. You just have to read it again and again. Take off your sandals, you are approaching holy ground!

### WHO WAS ZECHARIAH?

He was the grandson of the priest Iddo. Because of his family lineage, Zechariah was a priest. He was also called by God as a prophet. He, therefore, would have an intimate familiarity with the worship practices of the Jews, even if he had never served in a completed temple. He was born in captivity and grew up in exile in Babylon. The large caravan to Jerusalem with Zerubbabel was the first time he had come to the land of his heritage. The older prophet, Haggai, traveled with him on that long-anticipated return to the land of Israel. The two prophets ministered together in Jerusalem to rebuild the Temple and call the people back to God.

## THE BOOK OF ZECHARIAH

Zechariah is a monumental work. It has the power and grandeur of Isaiah and the burdens and compassionate lamentations of Jeremiah. It also includes the prophetic parables and visions of Ezekiel and the prophetic scope of Daniel. They sweep from Babylon to Persia to Greece to Rome and lead to a Lamb slain for the sins of the world. Zechariah contains the entire package. The book has three main divisions.

## Zechariah     Content of the 3 sections

**Chapters 1-6**

God gave the prophet 8 night visions to bring encouragement and instruction to the returned exiles. The Temple was to be rebuilt, the priesthood restored and great hope was revealed for the nation in the future.

**Chapters 7 & 8**

Zechariah answered questions from the people concerning religious matters of fasting and the type of worship that pleases God. The promise of a great new day for Israel is for all who will follow God in faith.

**Chapters 9-14**

Zechariah delivers two great oracles concerning: 1. The judgment of the nations who opposed Israel; 2. The protection and salvation of Israel; and 3. The prophecies concerning the coming Messiah as Savior and King.

It was a time of great sorrow and discouragement for the nation of Israel. This can be seen in the book of Lamentations which expresses the pain and the mood of the people of Israel during and after the captivity. Jerusalem had fallen, the temple was destroyed. The people were defeated, discouraged, depressed and felt abandoned by God.

> **"And he (Nebuchadnezzar) carried away all Jerusalem, and all the princes, and all the mighty men of valor, even ten thousand captives, and all the craftsmen and smiths: none remained, save the poorest sort of the people of the land."** (2 Kings 24:14)

This catastrophic event was the direct result of Israel's constant rebellion against God's Covenant even after God's persistent warnings. Surrounded by war, grief, and suffering, the people of Israel acknowledged their sin and cried out to God for restoration. You can hear the despair in the hearts of the people echoing in the words of the prophet, Jeremiah.

> **"You, O Lord, rule forever;**
> **Your throne is from generation to generation.**
> **Why do You forget us forever?**
> **Why do You forsake us so long?**
> **Restore us to You, O Lord, that we may be restored;**
> **Renew our days as of old,**
> **Unless You have utterly rejected us**
> **And are exceedingly angry with us."**
> (Lamentations 5:19-22)

Jeremiah told them the captivity would last 70 years and it did. Then after the 70-year Babylonian captivity ended, the King of Persia, Cyrus the Great, decreed that the captives were free to return to their homeland and rebuild their Temple.

# Three returns from the Captivity

## THE FIRST RETURN - RECONSTRUCTION AND ENCOURAGEMENT

The first return was in 535 B.C, when under Prince Zerubbabel, 50,000 of the Israelites returned to Jerusalem. They rebuilt the great altar and laid the foundations of the second Temple. This return included prophets, Haggai and Zechariah, and also Joshua the high priest. Israel finally had an official high priest, priests, and prophets, and a new governor in Zerubbabel. Best of all, they were on their way to having the Temple restored.

Sadly, the people soon became discouraged because of outside opposition and stopped rebuilding the Temple. Fifteen years passed. Then Haggai called the people back to work to complete the Temple in 520 B.C. Zechariah had his visions at that same time and continued his prophecies another two years. The people began to work again. The second Temple under Zerubbabel was completed in 515 B.C., five years after Haggai had first rebuked the Israelites. Zechariah encouraged the people during that time.

## THE SECOND RETURN - THE LAW AND ORDER

The second return was 77 years later in 458 B.C., when a company under Ezra, the scribe, returned from Babylon and led the people back to the Law of God and repentance. About 5,000 are estimated to have returned to Jerusalem in this company.

## THE THIRD RETURN - SAFETY AND SECURITY

The third wave of returnees was in 445 B.C., 90 years after the first group of returnees. It was led by Nehemiah, the cup-bearer of the King of Persia. He returned with a large company and military escort (Nehemiah 2:9) to rebuild the city walls of Jerusalem and the gates. Nehemiah was appointed by the King as governor of the Jerusalem region. He rallied the people and rebuilt all the damaged walls around Jerusalem in just 52 days. Safety and security returned. The people were no longer mocked by the nations as they were before.

## A MESSAGE OF MERCY AND ENCOURAGEMENT

Encouragement and mercy are clear messages that came to the people through Zechariah. His name is not an accident, the Hebrew meaning of his name is "God has remembered!" He was just what the people needed. They needed what Jeremiah had been telling them:

> **"For I know the plans I have for you," declares the LORD,**
> **"PLANS TO PROSPER YOU AND NOT TO HARM YOU, PLANS TO**
> **GIVE YOU HOPE AND A FUTURE."** (Jeremiah 29:11)

The theme of mercy runs through the entire book.

> **"Therefore, this is what the LORD says: 'I will return to**
> **Jerusalem with mercy, and there my house will be rebuilt.**
> **And the measuring line will be stretched out over**
> **Jerusalem,' declares the LORD Almighty."**
> (Zechariah 1:16 NIV)

> **"I will strengthen the house of Judah, and I will save the**
> **house of Joseph, and I will bring them back, because I**
> **have had compassion on them; and they will be as though**
> **I had not rejected them, for I am the Lord their God and I**
> **will answer them."** (Zechariah 10:6)

The source of this mercy was the "Lord of Hosts" (used 51 times by Zechariah). The God of heaven and earth, the great God who commanded all the armies of heaven had come back with a heart of compassion and mercy. It was just what the hurting nation needed to hear. God is Great and He had remembered His children!

## WHAT CAN WE LEARN TODAY FROM ZECHARIAH'S LIFE AND MESSAGE?

Sorrow for us may endure for the night but joy will come in the morning. God will judge sin in our lives but He is always on our side, even when we feel He is not there. His greatest desire for us is to bless us but we need to obey Him.

## ZECHARIAH REFERENCED IN THE NEW TESTAMENT

- Zechariah 1:8, see Revelation 6:1-8.
- Zechariah 3:2, see Jude 9.
- Zechariah 3:9, see Revelation 5:6.
- Zechariah 8:16, see Ephesians 4:25.
- Zechariah 9:9, see Matthew 21:5; John. 12:14ff.
- Zechariah 11:12ff, see Matthew 27:9ff.
- Zechariah 12:10, see John 19:37; Revelation1:7.
- Zechariah 13:7, see Matthew 26:31; Mark 14:27.
- Zechariah 14:11, see Revelation 22:3.

## THE DEATH OF ZECHARIAH ACCORDING TO JESUS

**"Therefore, behold, I am sending you prophets and wise men and scribes; some of them you will kill and crucify, and some of them you will scourge in your synagogues, and persecute from city to city, so that upon you may fall the guilt of all the righteous blood shed on earth, from the blood of righteous Abel to the blood of Zechariah, the son of Berechiah, whom you murdered between the temple and the altar."** (Matthew 23:34-35)

# Section One
## The Night Visions of Zechariah (1:7-6:15)

God had a message for the exiles who returned from the 70-year Babylonian captivity. He had always communicated to his people through His chosen prophets and now it was time for Zechariah to be heard. God gave Zechariah eight visions, one after another, to show Israel what was going to come in the next few years. Peace was returning to the land and the temple destroyed by Babylon was going to be rebuilt. Also, a new godly governor, Zerubbabel, was in charge. Israel's high priest, Joshua, was back along with the priests. Sacrifices were starting up again. The enemy nations around them were coming under the judgment of God and so much more.

The visions most likely came in one night but they could have been in a series of nights. They came quickly, and they were meant to inform, encourage, and call the people back to repentance. Each vision begins with the word, "then" which indicates rapid sequence, one right after another. The visions are unique and fascinating. There is no other book in the Bible quite like Zechariah with the full scope of its prophetic messages. Also, there are a large number of Messianic prophecies.

**These are the visions in the first six chapters of Zechariah**

1. God's Horsemen Patrolling the Earth.
2. The Four Horns and the Four Craftsmen.
3. The Man with the Measuring Line.
4. Joshua, the High Priest, and the Branch.
5. The Golden Lampstand and Olive Trees.
6. The Flying Scroll.
7. The Woman in the Ephah Basket.
8. The Four Chariots.

Before the night visions began, Zechariah had an important word from God. The people felt they had been forgotten, abandoned by God during the 70-year exile. God's first message to them was that they had never been forgotten.

# Zechariah 1

## A Call to Repentance and a Family Reunion (1:1-5)

[1] "In the eighth month of the second year of Darius, the word of the Lord came to Zechariah the prophet, the son of Berechiah, the son of Iddo saying, [2] "The Lord was very angry with your fathers. [3] Therefore say to them, 'Thus says the Lord of hosts, "Return to Me," declares the Lord of hosts, "that I may return to you," says the Lord of hosts. [4] "Do not be like your fathers, to whom the former prophets proclaimed, saying, 'Thus says the Lord of hosts, "Return now from your evil ways and from your evil deeds."' But they did not listen or give heed to Me," declares the Lord. [5] "Your fathers, where are they? And the prophets, do they live forever? 6 But did not My words and My statutes, which I commanded My servants the prophets, overtake your fathers? Then they repented and said, 'As the Lord of hosts purposed to do to us in accordance with our ways and our deeds, so He has dealt with us.'""

Luke 15 describes the loving heart of God when the prodigal son left the pigpen of life and returned home. God was waiting for His runaway son and ran to meet him and covered his filth with a family robe. He hugged him back into the family, not as a servant but as a son. Zechariah begins with God pleading His prodigal nation to *"Return to Me, that I may return to you."* These were words of hope to a troubled people.

- The land was still desolate after 70 years of neglect.
- The work to rebuild and restore was hard.
- They did not have a lot of money (Haggai 1:6) or manpower.
- They suffered crop failures and drought (Haggai 1:10-11).
- Hostile enemies resisted the work (Ezra 4:1-5).
- They remembered easier times in Babylon.

The nation of Israel had good reason to feel that God was far away. The first words Zechariah uttered were to a nation that had been waiting a long time to hear from God:

> **"'Return to Me,' declares the Lord of hosts, 'that I may return to you,' says the Lord of hosts.'"** (1:3)

After enduring a great trial, the Apostle Paul realized a great truth. When we are weakest, God is strong. Israel's situation looked hopeless, but that is often when God does His greatest works. The people of the land of Israel and the returning exiles needed that kind of great work of God. God answered by giving Zechariah eight night visions to show the people what was happening and what would yet happen.

**Principle** – God is always ready to give His children a fresh start.

# Night Vision 1
## God's Horsemen Patrolling the Earth.
## (1:7-11)

*Principle -* *Even when we feel most alone and abandoned, God is there and has His sentries, His watchmen patrolling the earth. His eyes run to and fro, nothing escapes His notice. He is ever watchful over His people.*

⁷ "On the twenty-fourth day of the eleventh month, which is the month Shebat, in the second year of Darius, the word of the LORD came to Zechariah the prophet, the son of Berechiah, the son of Iddo, as follows: ⁸ I saw at night, and behold, a man was riding on a red horse, and he was standing among the myrtle trees which were in the ravine, with red, sorrel and white horses behind him. ⁹ Then I said, "My lord, what are these?" And the angel who was speaking with me said to me, "I will show you what these are." ¹⁰ And the man who was standing among the myrtle trees answered and said, "These are those whom the LORD has sent to patrol the earth." ¹¹ So they answered the angel of the LORD who was standing among the myrtle trees and said, "We have patrolled the earth, and behold, all the earth is peaceful and quiet."

## GENERAL DESCRIPTION

This first vision is a message of hope for all the people. The 70-year captivity was over and finally, there was peace in the land. Prosperity and blessing would come when the people were obedient to God. God's eyes have always been on His children. His angels are constant watchmen over their activities, night and day. Patrolling the earth is not the same as simply seeing. It speaks about being diligent to keep the land and the people safe. It is like having a security detail on duty. In Revelation, God has four horsemen assigned to dispense judgments at that time, but these horsemen in Zechariah's vision were protecting angels with a different assignment.

Ancient kings relied on sentries and spies to assess their kingdoms and ride back to give reports. The angels in this vision had returned from their assignment and proclaimed the good news, *"all the earth is peaceful and quiet."* Cyrus the Great had decreed the end of the captivity and God's exiled people had started to come home. Zechariah was with the first group of returning exiles which included key people in governmental and spiritual leadership. It was a new start and the patrols have reported that all was well and peaceful.

The land had been decimated but the angel was standing among myrtle trees, a sign of coming prosperity again. Zechariah's first of the night visions began with a picture of hope and promise, the drought was over, recovery had begun.

The one identified as *"the angel of the Lord"* in verse 11 was a very high ranking angel of the Lord Himself (Genesis 16:7-13, Genesis 22:11-18, Exodus 2:3-9, Judges 2:1-4) The angel of the Lord was standing in a ravine where water flowed and he was standing in a grove of luscious myrtle trees. He announced that the famine in the land was over. The mercy of God was flowing like a river and the beauty and fragrance of the myrtle trees were coming back. The time of discipline was complete. God was there to welcome His children home and to hug them. They had never stopped being His children even during their rebellion and exile.

The myrtle tree, which is an evergreen, has always been an important tree to Israel and the middle east. The leaves are used for medicinal purposes for the healing of many afflictions. The fragrant myrtle oil is a skin balm. They are large leafy trees and normally grow in valleys and ravines where rivers flow or water is abundant. The grove of myrtle trees is a picture of returning prosperity and hope of a blessed future. In this beautiful image, the people must have felt that it was the beginning of healing, the healing of their nation. The future new earth in Revelation is described with a similar image. The trees on the banks of the river flowing from God's throne have leaves that are for the healing of the nations.

> **Myrtle trees: "Israel is not likened to a cedar of Lebanon, which is majestic, or an oak tree, which is strong. Having blossoms that emit a sweet fragrance when crushed, the myrtle illustrates the strange grace of Israel in affliction."** (James Montgomery Boice)

*Principle - God may have to discipline us at times but He always has His best in mind for us.*

## WHAT ABOUT THOSE HORSES?

The angel of the Lord was on a red horse and other riders were on horses of various colors, red, white and yellowish-brown. It is only speculation of what these colors mean. Since the colors of the horses and the purpose of the angels are very different from the Four Horsemen of the Apocalypse (Revelation 6:1-8) we cannot equate the two events. These horsemen angels were not executing judgment but were bringing great news of peace to the returning exiles.

Most likely the colors represent the differences of assignment and the purpose of the angels. We don't know what that means. In any case, it is a beautiful picture, one of authority and encouragement.

"Probably pointing out the different orders of angels in the heavenly host, which are employed by Christ in the defense of his Church. The different colors may point out the gradations in power, authority, and excellence, of the angelic natures which are employed between Christ and men." (Clarke)

# God proclaims His love for His people and the land. He was restoring them. (1:12-17)

12 "Then the angel of the Lord said, "O Lord of hosts, how long will You have no compassion for Jerusalem and the cities of Judah, with which You have been indignant these seventy years?" 13 The Lord answered the angel who was speaking with me with gracious words, comforting words. 14 So the angel who was speaking with me said to me, "Proclaim, saying, 'Thus says the Lord of hosts, "I am exceedingly jealous for Jerusalem and Zion. 15 But I am very angry with the nations who are at ease; for while I was only a little angry, they furthered the disaster." 16 Therefore thus says the Lord, "I will return to Jerusalem with compassion; My house will be built in it," declares the Lord of hosts, "and a measuring line will be stretched over Jerusalem."' 17 Again, proclaim, saying, 'Thus says the Lord of hosts, "My cities will again overflow with prosperity, and the Lord will again comfort Zion and again choose Jerusalem."'"

Verses 12-17 literally drip with mercy. Mercy, mercy, and more mercy. How Israel needed mercy! Mercy means not getting what we deserve. Think about it. The nation had been warned again and again that if they disobeyed God, they would face horrible consequences, but if they obeyed they would be blessed above all peoples. Leviticus 26 is a lengthy set of promises and warnings. History is clear. Israel chose to go against God and everything that happened to them was exactly what God warned would happen. The exiles knew they were guilty, experiencing what God warned, even their land had stopped producing crops.

What do people need who are in this condition? They deserve more judgment but God showed mercy. Instead of getting what they deserved, God poured out grace (that means getting what they don't deserve.)

It was the same message that another prophet who lived at the same time had been telling the people who were left behind during the captivity. Listen to the words of Jeremiah:

> **"'For I know the plans I have for you,' declares the Lord, 'plans to prosper you and not to harm you, plans to give you hope and a future. Then you will call on Me and come and pray to Me, and I will listen to you. You will seek Me and find me when you seek Me with all your heart.'"**
> (Jeremiah 29:11-13)

Zechariah told them in this passage that the Lord of Hosts (Lord over all in heaven and earth) had compassion on His covenant people. His words were "comforting and gracious." The Temple was going to be rebuilt. The cities would again overflow with prosperity and Jerusalem would again be the city of God instead of a place of mocking by the surrounding nations. For those nations who mocked and even made things worse for Israel while it was in distress, God would pour out His wrath on them.

Four years after this vision was given to the people, the rebuilt Temple was completed.

# Night Vision 2

## The Four Horns and the four Craftsmen (1:18-21)

¹⁸ "Then I lifted up my eyes and looked, and behold, *there were* four horns. ¹⁹ So I said to the angel who was speaking with me, "What are these?" And he answered me, "These are the horns which have scattered Judah, Israel, and Jerusalem." ²⁰ Then the LORD showed me four craftsmen. ²¹ I said, "What are these coming to do?" And he said, "These are the horns which have scattered Judah so that no man lifts up his head; but these *craftsmen* have come to terrify them, to throw down the horns of the nations who have lifted up *their* horns against the land of Judah in order to scatter it."

### GENERAL DESCRIPTION

This vision is a reminder that God knew the four nations that had terrorized Israel. He had raised up four builders who would establish the new Temple, bring back the Law and bring terror on those nations who would come under His judgment.

### THE IDENTITY OF THE FOUR HORNS

The four horns are clearly identified as four nations, or enemies, that had been responsible for the scattering of Judah. Horns are symbols of powers and nations in other books of the Bible like Daniel and Revelation. They signify strength like the horns of a great bull. Authority, destruction, and powerful influence are pictured in the horns.

In contrast to the nations that wanted to confuse, destroy, disband, and conquer, are the four craftsmen. These are defenders and builders, not destroyers. This pictures those who would fight against the enemies and be willing to help Israel get back on their feet. The enemies of Israel who felt they were invincible would fall. The main function of the craftsmen was to cause terror to come upon the enemies of God.

There are wide differences and speculations among Bible commentators concerning the identities of the horns and craftsmen. Here are a few:

- They are viewed as spiritual powers (they are viewed as the actors in the spiritual warfare of the ages, angels, and demons).
- They are viewed as physical nations and authorities (hostile nations vs friendly nations to Israel).
- They are viewed as key people like priests and prophets (People like Nebuchadnezzar, Cyrus, Daniel, and Ezra). They could also be actual carpenters and masons rebuilding the temple, literal craftsmen.
- They are viewed as ideas or ideologies (good forces and evil forces in the world).
- They are viewed in general terms. That which fights against the Kingdom of God and that which defends the Kingdom.

For every opposition (horns) to the plan of God, God has assigned an equal amount of the remedy (craftsmen). God's solution is always adequate.

Many commentators are in agreement that the horns represent powers or empires that stood against or came against Israel. The Biblical text indicates that these horns took part in scattering Israel, Judah, and Jerusalem, spreading the people of

Israel over the entire earth. Some see the four hostile nations as being both present and future. That would be Babylon, Persia, Greece, and Rome which align with the vision of Daniel chapter two, God's interpretation of Nebuchadnezzar's dream. Others see them from the historical era of Zechariah. That would mean the nations that caused the most trouble for Israel up to that time. Egypt, Assyria, Babylon or even the local Canaanite enemies. Nehemiah referred to local resistance to the building of the walls. In either case, the best answer to the identity of the four horns is the nations that have caused the most trouble for the people of God.

## THE IDENTITY OF THE FOUR CRAFTSMEN

The four horns are hostile nations and the four craftsmen, or blacksmiths that God will use to hammer the iron horns into powder. Many identify the "craftsmen" as friendly nations, yet they disagree on which nations they represent.

Since the number "four" is mentioned in each case, four horns, four craftsmen, then we can assume that specific nations or individuals are in focus. It is possible that since we live more than 2,500 years later than when this happened, we may not be able to identify the actors with much clarity. Let's dig a bit deeper if we can.

The word "craftsmen" indicates a builder, not a destroyer. They came with a measuring line (1:16), a tool that is used to lay a foundation. That was the assignment of Zerubbabel. In this vision, they came to rebuild what the horns had destroyed. They were used to bring the rule of God to the world.

As with the horns, there are differences in interpretation among the Christian community. Some see them as spiritual powers and quote Zechariah 4:6 *". . . not by might nor by strength, but by my Spirit, says the LORD of the armies."*

It is pretty much agreed upon that *"horns"* when used as symbols represent nations or larger, powerful regions. However, this new image, *"craftsmen,"* is more of a description of individuals, God-empowered special agents sent in to fix what was broken. In light of what we know of who God sent to rebuild the Temple and who God used to fix the country and heal the hearts of the discouraged people, the craftsmen may well have been referring to Zerubbabel the governor, Joshua the high priest, Ezra the Scribe, and Nehemiah the builder. It may also have been the prophets chosen to bring the message of hope and inspiration to the people. That list would include Haggai, Zechariah, Jeremiah and Daniel who influenced Cyrus to end the captivity and send the people back. The only description we have about these craftsmen is:

> **". . . these craftsmen have come to terrify them, to throw down the horns of the nations.** (Zechariah 1:21)

So, could four individuals cause such fear and concern that the opposing nations would become terrified? An illustration from Joshua may be helpful at this point. Joshua sent spies to Jericho to assess the city. The spies were sheltered by a harlot named Rahab. Rahab told the spies that the thought of the God of Heaven coming against them terrified the people of Jericho.

> **"Now before they lay down, she (Rahab) came up to them on the roof, and said to the men, 'I know that the Lord has given you the land, and that the terror of you has fallen on us, and that all the inhabitants of the land have melted away before you. For we have heard how the Lord dried up the water of the Red Sea before you when you came out of Egypt, and what you did to the two kings of the Amorites who were beyond the Jordan, to Sihon and Og, whom you utterly destroyed. When we heard it, our hearts melted**

**and no courage remained in any man any longer because of you; for the Lord your God, He is God in heaven above and on the earth beneath.'"** (Joshua 2:8-11)

When Zechariah came to Jerusalem, the city was in disarray, the temple was gone, the army was gone, the leadership was under Babylon's authority, hope was gone. The nations that defeated it were satisfied that Israel was a defeated people. They even mocked Israel.

## GOD WAS BACK IN TOWN!

Nothing would have been more defeating to the enemy nations than to have the exiles return with leadership, priests and prophets and craftsmen to start rebuilding the Temple. Just as the people of Jericho feared Israel because God was with them, now the newly empowered people have returned in the name of the Lord of Hosts, with craftsmen who had measured the temple and were rebuilding in His power. It struck terror into their hearts and sent them fleeing. They would no longer be fighting a discouraged, weakened people, but God Himself. It wasn't the four people that brought terror to the enemy nations. It was the God of heaven and earth who had sent them home to rebuild. That was the message of Zechariah to His people; God was back!

*Principle - Thank God when opposition comes (**horns**), because there are also carpenters (**craftsmen**) coming to bring them to ruin and to deliver us.*

> **"The work needs a man who, when he has his work to do, puts his whole strength into it, and beats away with his hammer, or cuts through the wood that lays before him with might and resolves. Rest assured, you who tremble for the work of God, that when the horns grow troublesome, the carpenters will be found."** (Spurgeon)

71

# Zechariah 2

## Night Vision 3

## The Man with the Measuring Line (2:1-5)

[1] "Then I lifted up my eyes and looked, and behold, there was a man with a measuring line in his hand. [2] So I said, "Where are you going?" And he said to me, "To measure Jerusalem, to see how wide it is and how long it is." [3] And behold, the angel who was speaking with me was going out, and another angel was coming out to meet him, [4] and said to him, "Run, speak to that young man, saying, 'Jerusalem will be inhabited without walls because of the multitude of men and cattle within it. [5] For I,' declares the Lord, 'will be a wall of fire around her, and I will be the glory in her midst.'"

### CONSTRUCTION BEGINS ON THE TEMPLE

An angel, measuring out the new Temple re-construction, has arrived. A promise is given that one day a great new Temple will come with room for everyone in a time of peace.

Construction on the second Temple had begun. Not only was it going to be rebuilt but God Himself was protecting the project with a wall of fire and His glory in the midst. Those were familiar words to the people whose ancestors had camped with God for 40 years in the Sinai desert, who had witnessed the Tabernacle with the Shakina glory of God shining in their midst and a pillar of fire lighting the desert sky. This protective canopy of God was their heavenly sentry protecting them from all enemies. Now, the Temple was being rebuilt and God would protect them with fire and glory.

Look, Israel, the Temple site is being measured right now by His angels!

This vision has two parts. The first is that God promises that the Temple will be rebuilt and His protection will be on the people again. History shows that this second temple lasted hundreds of years and was later reconstructed, even larger, by Herod the Great in the first century. The second part of the vision gives a much larger fulfillment, a long-term hope for the people. Let's read it:

# A Great Day is Coming for Israel (2:6-13)

[6] "Ho there! Flee from the land of the north," declares the Lord, "for I have dispersed you as the four winds of the heavens," declares the Lord. [7] "Ho, Zion! Escape, you who are living with the daughter of Babylon." [8] For thus says the Lord of hosts, "After glory, He has sent me against the nations which plunder you, for he who touches you, touches the apple of His eye. [9] For behold, I will wave My hand over them so that they will be plunder for their slaves. Then you will know that the Lord of hosts has sent Me. [10] Sing for joy and be glad, O daughter of Zion; for behold I am coming and I will dwell in your midst," declares the Lord. [11] "Many nations will join themselves to the Lord in that day and will become My people. Then I will dwell in your midst, and you will know that the Lord of hosts has sent Me to you. [12] The Lord will possess Judah as His portion in the holy land, and will again choose Jerusalem. [13] "Be silent, all flesh, before the Lord; for He is aroused from His holy habitation."

## ALLOW ME TO PARAPHRASE THESE VERSES:

Oh, Israel, God pleads, don't put your trust in Babylon, your former home for the past 70 years, but put it in Me. I will judge the people of the North, the Babylonians, for what they did to you. You are the apple of My eye and no nation who strikes you will succeed but will meet My wrath. When they strike you they strike Me. The Apostle Paul learned that lesson when asked by God, "Why are you persecuting me? My judgment against those who persecute you is just the beginning of what I am about to do. I am going to one day dwell in your midst again as I did in the wilderness and you will again know that I am the Lord of all. You will know My glory. Be sure of this, all the earth will be silent before Me.

**The big message was that God will always have a people, even if only a remnant, that will one day live with Him.**

## TO SUMMARIZE ZECHARIAH CHAPTER2

The man with the measuring line was going to "measure Jerusalem in order to take possession of it." One day a multitude will be living in Jerusalem protected by God Himself. And for those who had attached themselves to the sins of Babylon, flee. I am bringing destruction upon all the nations who are My enemies, who have touched the apple of My eye. (The Hebrew word translated "touch" is a word that also means "strike.") Here is how The Message Bible and one other Bible teacher translate the passage:

> **"God-of-the-Angel-Armies, the One of Glory who sent me on my mission, commenting on the godless nations who stripped you and left you homeless, said, 'Anyone who hits you, hits me—bloodies my nose, blackens my eye. Yes, and**

**at the right time I'll give the signal and they'll be stripped and thrown out by their own servants. Then you'll know for sure that God-of-the-Angel-Armies sent me on this mission.'"** (The Message, a Bible paraphrase)

**"Israel is precious to Almighty God, the apple [pupil] of His eye. He is simply saying, 'You touch my chosen nation Israel. You poke me in the eye.'"**
(Bible teacher, Grant Phillips)

A day is coming for all of true Israel when God will dwell in their midst. This vision describes God as being aroused from His patience and waiting. Now He has begun the final act of His program of reconciling His people to Himself. One day in the future, Judah will be God's possession in the land. This entire vision is a picture of the present and future hope for Israel.

# Zechariah 3

## THIS CHAPTER HAS TWO PARTS THAT ARE THE PROGRESSION OF ONE THEME, THE HIGH PRIEST AND ISRAEL.

- Joshua is the high priest in the time of Zechariah. This vision shows that God is restoring the priesthood to Israel after the 70-year exile.

- The Branch prophecy looks ahead to our Great High Priest who was foreshadowed by the Old Testament High Priest of Israel. We see our Messiah/High Priest in His glorified state when God will again dwell with His people in eternity future.

# Night Vision 4
## Joshua, the High Priest (3:1-7)

[1] "Then he showed me Joshua the high priest standing before the angel of the Lord, and Satan standing at his right hand to accuse him. [2] The Lord said to Satan, "The Lord rebuke you, Satan! Indeed, the Lord who has chosen Jerusalem rebuke you! Is this not a brand plucked from the fire?" [3] Now Joshua was clothed with filthy garments and standing before the angel. [4] He spoke and said to those who were standing before him, saying, "Remove the filthy garments from him." Again, he said to him, "See, I have taken your iniquity away from you and will clothe you with festal robes." [5] Then I said, "Let them put a clean turban on his head." So, they put a clean turban on his head and clothed him with garments, while the angel of the Lord was standing by. [6] And the angel of the Lord admonished Joshua, saying, [7] "Thus says the Lord of hosts, 'If you will walk in My ways and if you will perform My service, then you will also govern My house and also have charge of My courts, and I will grant you free access among these who are standing here."

## GENERAL DESCRIPTION

When the Temple was destroyed, the High Priest and the sacrifices were gone from the land for seventy years. Now, Joshua the High Priest, having returned from exile, is seen in soiled garments that picture the spiritual state of the people and their worship. God instructed Joshua to be cleaned and redressed. The message to the people was that God had returned and the temple and priesthood were being restored. It was time to clean the house.

## WE ARE INTRODUCED TO JOSHUA THE HIGH PRIEST.

> (Y⁰hôwshûwa', yeh-ho-shoo'-ah; *Jehovah-saved*;
> Jehoshua (i.e. Joshua), the Jewish leader:—Jehoshua,
> Jehoshuah, Joshua.)

An interesting stage is set in this vision. The Lord of Hosts is present along with two individuals standing before Him. There is the official High Priest, Joshua, who has come back with Zerubbabel's group of returning exiles. But he did not look like the former High Priest of Israel. His priestly garments were soiled and filthy. If we ever want to know how filthy our sins are to God, the Hebrew word translated "filthy" means "covered with human excrement." And standing next to him was Satan who was there to accuse him, which by the way is one of his job descriptions. He is the accuser of the brethren. There would be much to accuse. The prosecution would be easy; simply list the many sins of Israel and the failures of its leadership in the past. Israel had shamed the priesthood, the prophets, and God's calling many times. The evidence was overwhelming.

Before Satan could begin his prosecution, The Lord of Hosts ended the trial. Satan himself was condemned for his continuous attacks against God's chosen people. God reminded Satan of his place and his failure. Jerusalem was still standing and served as a rebuke to the schemes of the enemy. The High Priest may have been soiled and filthy but he was now back in right standing with God. God then instructed the angels to remove Joshua's soiled priestly garments. Then he was clothed with new garments which were spotless and beautiful: the white coat, the royal robe, the ephod, the golden chains, belts, precious stones, and the turban with the gold shield which said: *"holy unto the Lord."*

The clean priestly garments were lovingly placed on Joshua. The prodigal priest and nation had come home to their Father. The royal robe was placed on His prodigal people and there was much to celebrate.

The Lord of hosts reminded Satan that Israel was once a scrawny, burnt stick taken out of a fire. Now look at them! A nation rebuilding from the fire! When this vision was given to the people, the city was still a burnt-out shell of what it once was. Israel along with the priesthood and all hope were all like a burnt stick, but a stick that had been *plucked (rescued) from the fire.* To Joshua, the Lord had admonished him to walk worthy of this newly returned privilege. He was promised heavenly access to God and His hosts, and to spiritual authority to govern the new Temple. The house was clean and it was time for everyone to come home.

# The Branch Prophecy (3:8-10)

8 "Now listen, Joshua the high priest, you and your friends who are sitting in front of you—indeed they are men who are a symbol, for behold, I am going to bring in My servant the Branch. 9 For behold, the stone that I have set before Joshua; on one stone are seven eyes. Behold, I will engrave an inscription on it,' declares the Lord of hosts, 'and I will remove the iniquity of that land in one day. 10 'In that day,' declares the Lord of hosts, 'every one of you will invite his neighbor to sit under his vine and under his fig tree.'"

## GENERAL DESCRIPTION

There are many elements in this passage. We will examine each one.

- The "Branch."
- The stone with seven eyes.
- An engraving on the stone.
- Iniquity removed in a single day.
- A great day of peace.

## WHO IS THE "BRANCH?"

Joshua was told that he and the others with him were a "symbol." They not only symbolized the blessing of God on the restored priesthood but they would be a picture of a day in the future when the final High Priest would come. He is called the Branch in this vision. This One will be the ultimate Great High Priest and eternal advocate and mediator.

**Isaiah had prophesied about Him:**

> **"Who has believed our message**
> **and to whom has the arm of the Lord been revealed?**
> **He grew up before him like a tender shoot,**
> **and like a root out of dry ground.**
> **He had no beauty or majesty to attract us to him,**
> **nothing in his appearance that we should desire him.**
> **He was despised and rejected by mankind,**
> **a man of suffering, and familiar with pain.**
> **Like one from whom people hide their faces**
> **he was despised, and we held him in low esteem.**
> **Surely he took up our pain**
> **and bore our suffering,**
> **yet we considered him punished by God,**
> **stricken by him, and afflicted.**
> **But he was pierced for our transgressions,**
> **he was crushed for our iniquities;**
> **the punishment that brought us peace was on him,**
> **and by his wounds, we are healed."** (Isaiah 53:1-5 NIV)

This vision about Joshua, the High Priest, ended with a prediction of the coming Messiah, symbolized by a *"Branch."*

The office of the high priest was established in the time of Moses by God. He was designated as the spiritual head of Israel, and by divine design, foreshadowed the final Great High Priest to come, the Lord Jesus Christ.

The small, insignificant "tender shoot" Isaiah spoke of became the One who was pierced for our transgressions and crushed for our iniquities. He is the same Branch which is now seated at the right hand of the Father, our Great High Priest, and Intercessor who lives forever.

Since the Old Testament High Priest pointed ahead to Jesus Christ, our Great High Priest, it was important for God to rebuild Israel's high priest and system of worship after the captivity. Verse eight makes a clear reference to the fact that the Old Testament Priesthood was pointing out something coming in the future.

> [8] *"Now listen, Joshua the high priest, you and your friends who are sitting in front of you—indeed **they are men who are a symbol**, for behold, I am going to bring in My servant the Branch."*

When future events are described in prophetic passages (Apocalyptic writings), we will often encounter unusual descriptions that can seem confusing. Verse nine contains one such description.

## THE SEVEN EYED STONE

> **"'For behold, the stone that I have set before Joshua; on one stone are seven eyes. Behold, I will engrave an inscription on it,' declares the Lord of hosts, 'and I will remove the iniquity of that land in one day.'"**

This verse follows verse eight which introduces the Branch, a Messianic reference. The reign of the Messiah is a theme also of the final verse; verse 10. Therefore, it stands to reason that verse nine is also about the coming of the Messiah, the Branch.

Are there passages in the Bible relating to Christ that contain the following topics?

- A stone or rock
- Seven eyes
- The inscription on the stone
- Removal of the iniquity of Israel in one day

Yes, let's look at them.

## A STONE OR ROCK

**"Jesus said to them, Have you never read in the Scriptures, 'The stone which the builders rejected, this has become the head of the corner. This was from the Lord, and it is marvelous in our eyes'?"** (Matthew 21:42)

**"Being built upon the foundation of the apostles and prophets, Christ Jesus Himself being the cornerstone; in whom all the building, being fitted together, is growing into a holy temple in the Lord; in whom you also are being built together into a dwelling place of God in spirit. The Lord Jesus has become the cornerstone for the building of the church."**
(Ephesians 2:20-22)

**"Coming to Him, a living stone, rejected by men but with God chosen and precious, you yourselves also, as living stones, are being built up as a spiritual house into a holy priesthood to offer up spiritual sacrifices acceptable to God through Jesus Christ."** (1 Peter 2:4-5)

## SEVEN EYES

There is a reference in the Book of Revelation that describes the Holy Spirit as having seven eyes. He is also described as a seven-fold spirit. It is a picture of perfection. The vision John sees is a visual representation of the Trinity. The One on the throne and the Lamb of God next to Him and the Seven-fold Spirit are all part of the scene.

> **"And I saw in the midst of the throne and of the four living creatures and in the midst of the elders a Lamb standing as having just been slain, having seven horns and seven eyes, which are the seven Spirits of God."**
> (Revelation 5:6.)

## THE INSCRIPTION ON THE STONE

The Lord of Hosts engraved something on the stone. We aren't told what it was. It is possible it is the same phrase that was engraved on the golden plate on the forehead of the Old Testament High Priest, *"Holiness unto the Lord."*

The names of the 12 tribes were on stones the high priest bore on his garments. Maybe our names, His elect children, are engraved on our High Priest. It could be an engraving of God's ownership and character. We aren't sure.

Some think it is what John chapter1 is referring to, *"The Word was made flesh, and dwelt among us (and we beheld His glory, the glory as of the only begotten of the Father), full of grace and truth"* *(John 1:14).* God the Son was made flesh, carved into humanity, and we saw His engraving, His glory. These are just some of the many suggestions some commentators have made. We may not be able to fully understand this mystery yet.

It is encouraging for us to notice that on several occasions an angel asked Zechariah if he understood what he had seen and he said "No." Other prophets like Daniel had the same response. Daniel was even told that he would not be given the meaning because the time was not right.

> "As for me, I heard but could not understand; so I said, 'My lord, what will be the outcome of these events?' He said, 'Go your way, Daniel, for these words are concealed and sealed up until the end time.'"
>
> (Daniel 12:8, 9)

Even though there are things we can understand, there still are some secrets that will have to wait for another day. The inscription on the stone may remain a mystery for a while.

## INIQUITY REMOVED IN A DAY

The High Priest had several duties but one of the most important was to lead the people to national repentance on the annual Day of Atonement. It was a single day when the sins of the nation were forgiven through the sacrifices made for the nation and by faith in what God promised. It was an annual feast repeated year after year.

The prophecy of the Branch promises a greater day when sins will be totally removed in a single day, once for all. Jesus, our Great High Priest, went to the cross at Calvary and became the final Passover Lamb and paid for all sins once for all. It was "finished."

> "But the Messiah has appeared, high priest of the good things that have come. In the greater and more perfect tabernacle not made with hands (that is, not of this creation), He entered the most holy place once for all, not by the blood of goats and calves, but by His own blood, having obtained eternal redemption." (Hebrews 9:11, 12)
>
> "He doesn't need to offer sacrifices every day, as high priests do—first for their own sins, then for those of the people. He did this once for all when He offered Himself." (Hebrews 7:27)
>
> "By this will of God, we have been sanctified through the offering of the body of Jesus Christ once for all." (Hebrews 10:10)

# A DAY OF PEACE IS COMING

> "'In that day,' declares the Lord of hosts, 'every one of you
> will invite his neighbor to sit under his vine and under his
> fig tree.'" (3:10)

The final scene is set in the future when the Messiah returns.
It will be a time when the redeemed of Israel will recline with
friends and neighbors in peace, each man under his own vine
and fig tree. The wars will be over.

In the Jewish feast calendar, there were seven prescribed feasts
(Leviticus 23). They each served a purpose for the nation then,
but also by divine design pointed to the One who would one day
fulfill all of them. Christ, our sinless lamb, was sacrificed for us
and then rose from the dead. This fulfilled the feasts of
Passover, Unleavened Bread, and First Fruits. Then the fourth
feast, Pentecost, was fulfilled when Christ's Church was born.
The final three feasts all point to the time of the second coming
of Christ. The first four were fulfilled at His first coming.

The final feasts are Trumpets, Day of Atonement (which is a day
of fasting) and Tabernacles. Jesus will be coming again with a
loud trumpet blast, and as we have seen, He is our ultimate Day
of Atonement, judging all sin. All of it will be finished. The only
remaining feast is Tabernacles which the Jews love to celebrate
even to this day. The feast is a remembrance of when God
delivered His people from slavery in Egypt and camped with
Israel in the wilderness. And He had His own tent, the
Tabernacle. The feast of Tabernacles remembers that time and
looks forward to a future day when God's people will dwell with
Him again.

> "In that day,' declares the Lord of hosts, 'every one of you
> will invite his neighbor to sit under his vine and under his
> fig tree.'" (3:10)

# Zechariah 4

## The Golden Lampstand and Olive Trees

Zechariah was a priest and Joshua was the high priest. Both of them were very familiar with the various pieces of furniture in the Holy Place in the Temple. The Lampstand was one of those items. One of the priestly duties performed in the Temple was maintaining the seven-branched lampstand. It took continual refilling of the lamp oil and trimming the wicks. The description of the Lampstand, the oil used, and the duties of the priests, were clearly given in the writings of Moses.

The vision God gave Zechariah of the Lampstand was quite different from the one described in the Law of Moses. The vision confused Zechariah and he had to ask the angel two times about the meaning of what he had seen.

## Not by might but by God's power (4:1-6)

[1] "Then the angel who was speaking with me returned and roused me, as a man who is awakened from his sleep. [2] He said to me, "What do you see?" And I said, "I see and behold, a lampstand all of gold with its bowl on the top of it, and its seven lamps on it with seven spouts belonging to each of the lamps which are on the top of it; [3] also two olive trees by it, one on the right side of the bowl and the other on its left side." [4] Then I said to the angel who was speaking with me saying, "What are these, my lord?" [5] So the angel who was speaking with me answered and said to me, "Do you

not know what these are?" And I said, "No, my lord." [6] Then he said to me, "This is the word of the Lord to Zerubbabel saying, 'Not by might nor by power, but by My Spirit,' says the Lord of hosts."

An interesting detail is revealed in verse one about the visions themselves. Zechariah indicated that after the previous vision he was in a trance type of mental state. He wasn't asleep or clearly awake. When the angel came back to give him the next vision he was roused, or stirred back into awareness, like a person who has awakened from sleep. These visions were non-stop and stunning, almost mind-numbing, experiences. They were certainly other-world events that could leave a person in a state of mental suspension, between heaven and earth. The angel had to get Zechariah's attention to begin the fifth vision.

This vision is a message for the governor, Zerubbabel. He was charged with rebuilding the Temple. The purpose of this message to him was to encourage him that it would be done by the power of God, not by the might and power of Zerubbabel. It is God who would remove all the obstacles. It also let him know that this reconstruction was part of a much larger purpose that God has for the future. Zerubbabel was not just rebuilding a temple but was part of a much bigger event.

> **"Verses 4:1-14: The fifth vision, the golden 'candlestick' and the 'two olive trees': The work of God (the rebuilding of the temple), would be accomplished through God's leaders, Joshua and Zerubbabel, who would be enabled to perform their tasks by the Spirit of God."**

> **"The vision indicates that future Israel will be a blessing to all the nations of the world through an abundant supply of the Spirit of God as the result of the coming of the Messiah, who will unite the offices of priest and king in Himself."** (Bible.org)

## THE CONFUSING LAMPSTAND IN THE VISION

There are significant differences between the lampstand in the original Temple and the one in the vision with the two olive trees. There is a large central bowl, a system of pipes and two living olive trees supplying oil directly to the burning lamps. The general meaning is not that difficult but the identity of the two olive trees is a much larger challenge. We will get to that.

The general message is that the old system would one day be replaced and it would be accomplished by God, not man. Howeverbefore that day came, Zerubbabel would be the one to rebuild the new Temple and he would need the power of God to accomplish that task. God promised Zerubbabel that He, the all-powerful God, would be there with him to see the job finished. It would not be done by human might but by the power of God.

There would be many challenges to face. They are described as a great mountain and a lot of rubble.

## THE GREAT MOUNTAIN – RUBBLE AND TROUBLE (4:7)

7 'What are you, O great mountain? Before Zerubbabel you will become a plain; and he will bring forth the top stone with shouts of "Grace, grace to it!"'"

It was a great encouragement to Zechariah to know that God was an active participant in the rebuilding of the Temple and the nation that would one day introduce the Messiah to the world. First, there was a mountain of challenge in front of him. Here is what one commentator sees in that image:

> *"Who are you, O great mountain? Before Zerubbabel, you shall become a plain!* The work of rebuilding the temple was so massive it seemed like a **great mountain**. Here God promised that by His Spirit, that **great mountain** would be leveled into a **plain**." (David Guzik)

When Nebuchadnezzar destroyed the temple of Solomon and the city of Jerusalem, one can only imagine what a large pile of rubble was left behind. To the discouraged Jews who remained in the land for 70 years without leadership, a temple, or priests, it was a constant pile of pulverized dreams the size of a mountain. The people had lost their hearts to work. God was telling them that a new Spirit had returned and would remove their mountain so the new temple could be built.

The passage goes on to say that Zerubbabel would complete the temple until the final capstone was put in place and all would see the message of it, Grace, Grace, it was all of grace.

Someone once said the key to overcoming adversity and discouragement is to keep two rules in mind.

> **Rule 1 - Don't sweat the small stuff.**
> **Rule 2 - It is all small stuff!**

To God, it is all small stuff. He created everything. Zerubbabel did accomplish all that God said he would. Verses 8-10 proclaim a similar message, this time to the people of Israel.

## ZERUBBABEL BEGAN THE WORK AND HE COMPLETED IT (4:8-10)

8 "Also, the word of the Lord came to me, saying, 9 "The hands of Zerubbabel have laid the foundation of this house, and his hands will finish it. Then you will know that the Lord of hosts has sent me to you. 10 For who has despised the day of small things? But these seven will be glad when they see the plumb line in the hand of Zerubbabel—these are the eyes of the Lord which range to and fro throughout the earth."

The progress had been slow and it seemed like opposition and discouragement had taken the heart out of the people. They had made only small progress. But that was about to change. Things were going to really get moving. They had learned the lesson that might and power alone would not complete the task, God would make sure the job got done.

**Principle** – The rocks and rubble that discouraged the people were just that, a lot of small things. Together, they looked like a mountain. Our life challenges are often similar. With God's help, you can clear the rocks, one at a time. Ministry can become overwhelming but often it is a series of difficult relationships, false accusations, disappointments with people, etc. Don't give up, just begin, one rock at a time. Each solved issue gets you closer to seeing that mountain knocked down. Each is still a victory.

## GOD, THE ALL-SEEING PROJECT MANAGER

The number "seven" often means perfection and completeness when it is used of God. In this passage, the "seven" who rejoice are explained as the eyes of the Lord. God has perfect vision and wisdom; nothing escapes His notice and care.

> **"But these seven will be glad when they see the plumb line in the hand of Zerubbabel—these are the eyes of the Lord which range to and fro throughout the earth."** (4:10)

> **"For the eyes of the Lord move to and fro throughout the earth that He may strongly support those whose heart is completely His."** (2 Chronicles 16:9)

God was pleased that Zerubbabel was busy with the rebuilding of the Temple. He was a working governor, with a plumb line in his hand. Zerubbabel was a dedicated, godly leader that was not afraid to get his hands dirty. It was a beautiful picture of the people and God together doing His work and working for His kingdom.

# The Two Olive Trees (4:11-14)

<sup>11</sup> Then I said to him, "What are these two olive trees on the right of the lampstand and on its left?" <sup>12</sup> And I answered the second time and said to him, "What are the two olive branches which are beside the two golden pipes, which empty the golden *oil* from themselves?" <sup>13</sup> So he answered me, saying, "Do you not know what these are?" And I said, "No, my lord." <sup>14</sup> Then he said, "These are the two anointed ones who are standing by the Lord of the whole earth."

Many times, we feel like Zechariah when he was asked if he understood what the olive trees and branches represented. His answer was *"No, my lord."* The angel of the Lord gave an explanation:

> "then he said, 'These are the two anointed ones, who stand beside the Lord of the whole earth.'" (4:14)

We know these two olive trees represent two people or two angels. As with many of the visions, there are differing views about the identity of the two olive trees. One passage that cannot be avoided is found in Revelation chapter 11.

## THE SIMILARITY OF LANGUAGE AND IMAGES WITH REVELATION 11

> "Then there was given me a measuring rod like a staff; and someone said, 'Get up and measure the temple of God and the altar, and those who worship in it. Leave out the court which is outside the temple and do not measure it, for it has been given to the nations; and they will tread under foot the holy city for forty-two months. And I will grant authority to my two witnesses, and they will prophesy for twelve hundred and sixty days, clothed in sackcloth.' These are the two olive trees and the two lampstands that stand before the Lord of the earth."
> (Revelation 11:1-4)

Zechariah seems to be talking specifically about two people in his day who were chosen, that stand before the Lord, to be the ones that bring about God's plan to restore His Temple and the nation. It is also possible that the two he had in mind will prefigure an event yet to happen in the last days. It may even be the same two people. The vision may have a present purpose and also a future fulfillment.

The two anointed ones in the day of Zechariah were Governor Zerubbabel and Joshua, the High Priest. They both held very privileged positions, King and Priest. One rebuilt the land and the Temple and the other was the spiritual head of the nation for the first time since the captivity. God throughout Scripture has a Redemptive plan and a Kingdom plan. He will redeem His people and He will reign over His creation. Zerubbabel and Joshua were branches from the Olive trees, not the olive trees themselves. The real source of oil and eternal light is the One who is both Redeemer and King, Jesus Christ.

God will one day raise up two witnesses before Christ returns who will preach to the rebellious earth and call people back to the way of God. Are they the same two people? I think it may be best to stick with Zechariah's answer, "I don't know." But it seems that both sets of anointed servants were branches from the main olive tree. He is the source of the ever-flowing oil. All the events the visions describe ultimately find their source in God. None of it is by might, or by power, but by the Spirit of God.

**Summary of the two visions, Joshua and the branch, and the Golden Lampstand and two Olive Trees.**

Both of these visions make one complete message. God had not forgotten His people. He was restoring the priesthood and the Temple. He was forgiving His people and cleaning them up. God would be the One to sustain His people. He had chosen and sent some special servants to accomplish His will on earth, Zerubbabel and Joshua.

Zechariah's lampstand differed from the Old Testament Lampstand in the Temple in four ways:

- A bowl
- Pipes
- Olive trees
- Two golden spouts

The Lampstand was a very familiar image to the Jewish people but this one was a kind of expanded version. The vision indicated that there was a future, more complete, picture yet to come. We were introduced in the former vision to the "Branch," which pointed to the future Messiah. This vision is similar in that it tells a present story for the time of the exiles and points to something yet to come, or Someone yet to come. The light in the Old Testament Temple system came from the lampstand which required constant maintenance from the priests. The new picture of the lampstand had a perpetual supply of oil coming directly from the two olive trees through a system of pipes and bowls. Every part of this vision is based on the power of God. All of it will be accomplished by the Spirit of God, not by human might or power. The message to Zerubbabel was that he would complete the rebuilding of the Temple but he was also part of a larger story in the entire saga of Israel. It is the story of God one day living with and sustaining His people.

# Zechariah 5

## Night Vision 6
### The Flying Scroll (5:1-4)

[1]"Then I lifted up my eyes again and looked, and behold, there was a flying scroll. [2] And he said to me, "What do you see?" And I answered, "I see a flying scroll; its length is twenty cubits and its width ten cubits." [3] Then he said to me, "This is the curse that is going forth over the face of the whole land; surely everyone who steals will be purged away according to the writing on one side, and everyone who swears will be purged away according to the writing on the other side. [4] I will make it go forth," declares the Lord of hosts, "and it will enter the house of the thief and the house of the one who swears falsely by My name; and it will spend the night within that house and consume it with its timber and stones."

### GENERAL DESCRIPTION

This vision was about the wickedness in the land of Israel which was being judged and removed. The Law of God had been broken and brought condemnation to the people.

A large scroll was seen flying through the air. It is interesting that the size of the scroll was identical to the size of the Holy Place in the Tabernacle in the Wilderness. The sins of the people were written on both sides of it. This scroll, which pictured the Law of God, contained a curse on all the evil Israel had done against God and neighbor. The people who had covenanted with God had broken their promises. They had stolen from God. The prophet Malachi would also tell them that.

93

They used the wood and materials designated for the Temple to beautify their homes. The prophet Haggai warned them of that sin. They had married foreign women from Babylon and the pagan nations around Israel. Ezra will help bring them back to the Law of God, repent as a nation and put away the ungodly wives they had accumulated. In all, the land of Israel had just come through a seventy-year discipline of God and yet they still had not learned all the lessons. Zechariah was given the vision of the flying scroll to teach the people that God's broken Law was now seeking out and exposing the sin of the land.

The sins listed in this vision were lying to God and man and stealing. This is generally viewed in one of two ways. The first is that God is specifically focusing on these two violations. The people had been using the materials designated for the rebuilding of the temple to make their own houses more luxurious (Haggai 1:2-6). They had also stolen from God by not tithing (Malachi 3:8-10). Some see this vision as specifically dealing with those two listed sins.

Others see the two sins as representing the entire broken law. The moral law of God has two themes. The laws in commandments 1-4 relate to man's relationship with God. The last six relate to man's relationship with his neighbor

> **"Jesus said unto him, 'Thou shalt love the Lord thy God with all thy heart, and with all thy soul, and with all thy mind. This is the first and great commandment. And the second is like, unto it, Thou shalt love thy neighbor as thyself. On these two commandments hang all the law and the prophets.'"** (Matthew 22:37-40).

Since the overall sins of the people extended beyond lying and stealing, it was most likely a vision of condemnation on a people who had violated their relationship with God and their neighbor. They stood totally condemned. In the vision, The Law of God goes house to house exposing the sin of the people.

> **"'I will make it go forth,' declares the Lord of hosts, 'and it will enter the house of the thief and the house of the one who swears falsely by My name; and it will spend the night within that house and consume it with its timber and stones.'"** (4:4)

Jesus would later tell the Pharisees the same message. There is no escape from the judgment of God.

> **"Accordingly, whatever you have said in the dark will be heard in the light, and what you have whispered in the inner rooms will be proclaimed upon the housetops."** (Luke 12:3)

For God to bless His people, we need to repent. Sin must be removed from our lives just as the leaven was removed from the Jewish homes in the feast of the Unleavened Bread in Leviticus 23. This is the message of the next vision, the woman in the ephah basket. It is a timeless message, which is still very relevant today.

# Night Vision 7

## The Woman in the Ephah Basket (5:5-11)

5 "Then the angel who was speaking with me went out and said to me, "Lift up now your eyes and see what this is going forth." 6 I said, "What is it?" And he said, "This is the ephah going forth." Again he said, "This is their appearance in all the land 7 (and behold, a lead cover was lifted up); and this is a woman sitting inside the ephah." 8 Then he said, "This is Wickedness!" And he threw her down into the middle of the ephah and cast the lead weight on its

opening. [9] Then I lifted up my eyes and looked, and there two women were coming out with the wind in their wings; and they had wings like the wings of a stork, and they lifted up the ephah between the earth and the heavens. [10] I said to the angel who was speaking with me, "Where are they taking the ephah?" [11] Then he said to me, "To build a temple for her in the land of Shinar; and when it is prepared, she will be set there on her own pedestal."

## GENERAL DESCRIPTION

The message of this vision continues the theme of wickedness that had come into the land. God's people had brought a curse on the land. When the people returned from captivity, they had become soiled from the High Priest to the everyday person. They had become polluted with the sins of the pagan nations. These sins needed to be removed far from them. Two demonic angels symbolically carried the evil back to Babylon in a basket.

The basket is a common basket that held an "ephah" amount of grain (about seven gallons). The basket, we commonly call a "bushel basket," was simply called an "ephah."

## DEFINITIONS

**Ephah** - Hebrew unit of dry measure, equal to about a bushel (35 liters). A bushel basket.

**Shinar** - the term used in the Hebrew Bible for the general region of Mesopotamia, which included Babylon.

The exiled people learned many new things while in captivity. Mostly a farming people, many had become business owners and merchants while living in Babylon. They also lived in a land of great idolatry and had become compromised. Daniel told of a time when everyone bowed to a great gold image, except for only three who honored God and refused to bow.

"Therefore at that time, when all the peoples heard the sound of the horn, flute, lyre, trigon, psaltery, bagpipe and all kinds of music, all the peoples, nations and men of every language fell down and worshiped the golden image that Nebuchadnezzar the king had set up." (Daniel 3:7)

Idolatry, lying, stealing, the exiles brought many things back with them that had to be put away. This vision is saying that the land of their heritage and the Temple had no place for these sins. The evil needed to go back and stay in the land of Babylon. Just as a stork is known to return to its nest, so the angels with stork wings will carry the wickedness back to its own home, Babylon.

The wickedness of Israel is symbolized by a woman in a bushel basket. A woman is used to personify evil in the book of Revelation.

"The woman was clothed in purple and scarlet, and adorned with gold and precious stones and pearls, having in her hand a gold cup full of abominations and of the unclean things of her immorality, and on her forehead a name was written, a mystery, 'BABYLON THE GREAT, THE MOTHER OF HARLOTS AND OF THE ABOMINATIONS OF THE EARTH.'" (Revelation 17:4, 5)

The land of Israel had been under a curse for 70 years and the abundant grain from the past has now been replaced with wickedness. The basket which should have been full of grain was filled with sins of idolatry, lying and stealing.

A lead lid was put on the basket of sins and it was carried back to the land of its origin. The lead lid was thick and heavy and the message was that nothing in that basket was ever to escape and pollute the land of Israel again.

## THE TWO ANGELS GOD USED IN THIS VISION WERE UNUSUAL.

They weren't described in words we normally associate with Heavenly angels. The wings described are stork wings. Their job was to return the sins of Babylon back home where they belong. Storks in Leviticus are an unclean animal, forbidden to be eaten.

> **"These, moreover, you shall detest among the birds; they are . . . the stork, the heron in its kinds, and the hoopoe, and the bat."** (Leviticus 11:13, 19)

Why would God use a detestable animal to describe the wings of the two angels who carried the wickedness of the land back to pagan Babylon? They seem to be a description, not of heavenly angels, but fallen angels who have been called to pick up their vile sins and take them back where they belong.

> **"Two women ... wind was in their wings": Since storks are unclean birds** (Lev. 11:19; Deut. 14:18), **these must be agents of evil. Demonic forces, protective of the wicked secularism, who set up the final system of evil. God allowed them to set up the world system that the Lord will destroy when He returns** (Rev. 19:11-16)."
> (David Guzik, Blue Letter Bible)

The fact that the sins were to be carried to Babylon and enshrined there is an indicator that the sins were originally imported from there. The older word for Babylon is used, "Shinar." Shinar is associated with one of the earliest rebellions against God which resulted in God confounding the languages of the people on earth.

> **"Now Cush became the father of Nimrod; he became a mighty one on the earth. He was a mighty hunter before the Lord; therefore it is said, 'Like Nimrod a mighty hunter before the Lord.' The beginning of his kingdom was Babel and Erech and Accad and Calneh, in the land of Shinar."** (Genesis 10:8-10)

The message to the people was strong. Their sin had become like the sin of Shinar, it was a rebellion against God. It was time to rid the land of evil. Wicked spirits have been called in the vision to come, pick up the evil of Shinar and take it home and return it to a pagan temple where it can be worshipped there, but not in Israel.

For us today the message is the same. We may be in the world but we must never accept the ways of the world to pollute or compromise our walk with Christ.

# Zechariah 6

## Night Vision 8
### The Four Chariots (6:1-8)

¹"Now, I lifted up my eyes again and looked, and behold, four chariots were coming forth from between the two mountains; and the mountains *were* bronze mountains. ² With the first chariot *were* red horses, with the second chariot black horses, ³ with the third chariot white horses, and with the fourth chariot strong dappled horses. ⁴ Then I spoke and said to the angel who was speaking with me, "What are these, my lord?" ⁵ The angel replied to me, "These are the four spirits of heaven, going forth after standing before the Lord of all the earth, ⁶ with one of which the black horses are going forth to the north country; and the white ones go forth after them, while the dappled ones go forth to the south country. ⁷ When the strong ones went out, they were eager to go to patrol the earth." And He said,

"Go, patrol the earth." So, they patrolled the earth. [8] Then He cried out to me and spoke to me saying, "See, those who are going to the land of the north have appeased My wrath in the land of the north."

## GENERAL DESCRIPTION

This vision begins in a similar fashion as chapterone. We have angels and multicolored horses. They were patrolling the earth in the first vision. They were described as scouts on horseback patrolling the land and bringing back a report. However, in this last of the night visions, we see the angels driving chariots, vehicles of war. The first vision was meant to encourage people to work because God had come back to His people. This vision is meant to instill hope that a great victory and future were coming. God would punish Israel's enemies.

Babylon was later defeated by Persia. There was peace in the land and Joshua the High priest had a special crown put on his head. This vision looks ahead to the final Great High Priest who is also the King over Israel. God will complete all that He has promised.

Since the four colors of the horses in this vision are the same as the four horsemen of the Apocalypse in Revelation six, and since the purpose in both situations is bringing judgment on the earth, it is safe to assume they are connected. It may be that these particular angels of judgment are used in the time of Zechariah and again at the end of time. If that is the case then the colors would have a similar meaning in each case.

## THE MEANINGS OF THE HORSE COLORS IN REVELATION SIX

- **Rider on the White Horse – Conquest –** "I looked, and behold, a white horse, and he who sat on it had a bow; and a crown was given to him, and he went out conquering and to conquer." (Revelation 6:2)

- **Rider on the Red Horse – War** - "it was granted to take peace from the earth, and that *men* would slay one another; and a great sword was given to him." (Revelation. 6:4)

- **Rider on the Black Horse – Famine** – "I looked, and behold, a black horse; and he who sat on it had a pair of scales in his hand. And I heard *something* like a voice in the center of the four living creatures saying, 'A quart of wheat for a denarius, and three quarts of barley for a denarius; and do not damage the oil and the wine.'" (Revelation 6:5,6)

- **Rider on the Ashen Horse – Death** - "I looked, and behold, an ashen horse; and he who sat on it had the name Death; and Hades was following with him. Authority was given to them over a fourth of the earth, to kill with sword and with famine and with pestilence and by the wild beasts of the earth." (Revelation 6:8)

The angels in Zechariah six were agents of judgment and destruction. The first horses in Zechariah near the Myrtle trees were scouts telling of peace in the land. The horses and chariots in Zechariah six are battle-ready. When Zechariah asks the meaning, he is told:

> **"The angel replied to me, 'These are the four spirits of heaven, going forth after standing before the Lord of all the earth,'"** (6:5)

The vision is referring to angels who have assignments from God. The colors of the horses and chariots give meaning to the roles the angels play. They are sentries, conquerors, etc. They have been assigned different regions in the South and North. All armies and nations against Israel invaded from either the North or South. These angels are the ones who executed His will. The images of chariots and horses speak of the swiftness and military nature of the assignment.

The Lord tells us that the destruction on the north, or Babylon, has satisfied His wrath. Babylon was a war machine that was completely defeated by the Persian Empire. Cyrus of Persia ended the captivity bringing peace to the exiles. The mountains where the chariots came from were bronze, which was an Old Testament symbol of judgment. The war-chariots of God were coming from the bronze mountains of judgment.

> **"Then He cried out to me and spoke to me saying, 'See, those who are going to the land of the north have appeased My wrath in the land of the north.'"** (6:8)

Invading armies from the Persian world always came by way of the Fertile Crescent and traveled in from the North. Even though they are located to the North/East of Israel they are described as coming from the north.

Ezekiel told of the great judgment God was sending on Israel from Babylon. He described it as a storm approaching from the North. In Ezekiel's vision, God was pictured as an unstoppable war machine in fire and glory. Ezekiel was relaying the awesome power of God and His sovereign choice to accomplish His will by using Babylon as His instrument to judge the sins of Israel.

> **"As I looked, behold, a storm wind was coming from the north, a great cloud with fire flashing forth continually and a bright light around it, and in its midst something like glowing metal in the midst of the fire."** (Ezekiel 1:4)

The big picture for Israel was that God's armies were on their side and He was mobilizing them to defeat all their enemies, North and South. It would be as if having neighbors living on each side of you that continually caused trouble for your family. They gossiped about you and their children bullied your children. Then one day, the entire military of your government rolled down your street with armored vehicles and sirens. Then the General of the army, in view of your neighbors, walked up to your door and said, "I understand you could use some help!"

## AN OFFERING FOR THE TEMPLE RECONSTRUCTION (6:9, 10)

[9] "The word of the Lord also came to me, saying, [10] "Take an offering from the exiles, from Heldai, Tobijah, and Jedaiah; and you go the same day and enter the house of Josiah the son of Zephaniah, where they have arrived from Babylon."

A small group of exiles had arrived from Babylon with money raised for the Temple reconstruction. Zechariah was given instructions about the handling of the funds. It was generally accepted that the funds were to be given to Josiah, a resident and probably a treasurer of the Temple project. The purpose of this offering was to make a special, ornate crown to put on the head of the High Priest, Joshua. What was the reason for that? This question is answered in the final part of the last vision starting in verse 11.

## THE SYMBOLIC CROWN POINTS TO OUR FUTURE ETERNAL KING (6:11-15)

[11] "Take silver and gold, make an ornate crown and set it on the head of Joshua the son of Jehozadak, the high priest. [12] Then say to him, 'Thus says the Lord of hosts, "Behold, a man whose name is Branch, for He will branch out from where He is; and He will build the temple of the Lord. [13] Yes, it is He who will build the temple of the Lord, and He who will bear the honor and sit and rule on His throne. Thus, He

will be a priest on His throne, and the counsel of peace will be between the two offices."' [14] Now the crown will become a reminder in the temple of the Lord to Helem, Tobijah, Jedaiah, and Hen the son of Zephaniah. [15] Those who are far off will come and build the temple of the Lord." Then you will know that the Lord of hosts has sent me to you. And it will take place if you completely obey the Lord your God."

> **"This is one of the most remarkable and precious Messianic prophecies, and there is no plainer prophetic utterance in the whole Old Testament as to the Person of the promised Redeemer, the offices He was to fill, and the mission He was to accomplish."** (D. Baron)

Just as the garments of the priests and the high priest were designed by God in Moses' time to send a message to the people of God, so this crown also sent a message. Kings rule on a throne, priests serve with the people.

A special crown of gold and silver was to be made for the High Priest, Joshua. The request was an unusual request because high priests were not to wear crowns. They had a band of gold placed on their turbans but no crown. Crowns were reserved for kings and royalty. The first time Joshua was seen in the visions he was clothed in filthy garments but the Lord had him cleaned up and new garments put on him. The Temple was under construction and the nation needed a restored priesthood to again offer sacrifices for sin. We understand today that the entire system was a shadow of the final sacrifice to come, Jesus Christ. Jesus was clearly depicted in Hebrews as our final Great High Priest. Jesus was not just a Great High priest but He is also our King of kings and Lord of lords.

Jesus fulfilled all of the Biblical prophecies concerning God's redemptive work (purchasing our salvation). He will also fulfill all of the Biblical prophecies concerning God's Kingdom. He will reign forever as our King. He is both priest and king. That is why Joshua the high priest had a crown put on his head. It helped the people see the larger picture of what was coming. The Messiah to come would be both the solution for the sin of man and would also reign forever as our King of kings. This picture also completes the message of the two covenants God made with Israel. As a High Priest, Joshua was in the line of the Abrahamic Covenant (Salvation provided to bless the world). The crown connected him to the Davidic Covenant (The eternal one that will reign in all eternity from the line of David).

When the One who was foreshadowed in this vision first appears in the New Testament, read how He was introduced:

> **"The record of the genealogy of Jesus the Messiah, the son of David, the son of Abraham."** (Matthew 1:1)

If there is any question that this is describing the future King and High Priest, look again at verses 12 and 13. We have already seen the "Branch" as a prophetic description of the coming Messiah in Isaiah and Jeremiah. It is also important to note that the root meaning of the names "Joshua" and "Jesus" are the very same, "The Lord saves."

> **"Then say to him, 'Thus says the Lord of hosts, "Behold, a man whose name is Branch, for He will branch out from where He is; and He will build the temple of the Lord. Yes, it is He who will build the temple of the Lord, and He who will bear the honor and sit and rule on His throne. Thus, He will be a priest on His throne, and the counsel of peace will be between the two offices."'"**
> (6:12, 13)

**"Along with Psalm 110, this verse is one of the clearest statements in the Old Testament that the coming Davidic king would also be a priest."** (Chisholm)

Verses 12-15 teach several things about the Branch, the Messiah, Jesus:

- He will come from Israel (12).
- He will build the millennial temple (12b, 13a).
- He will be glorious (13).
- He will be king and priest (13).
- He makes peace (13).
- He opens the kingdom to Gentiles (15a).
- He will corroborate God's Words (15b).
- He demands obedience (15c).

For further information about our Great High Priest, please refer to the book of Hebrews in the New Testament.

**This completes Section One, the visions of Zechariah. Next, the prophet will answer several questions and concerns of the people in chapters seven and eight. Finally, he will give two large Messianic proclamations in chapters 9-14.**

# Section Two
## Questions about Fasting and Feasting
# Chapters Seven and Eight

Two years have passed since Zechariah's night visions. A small group of delegates arrived in Jerusalem from Bethel, about ten miles away. They said they had been faithful in fasting and living the way God wanted but what they wanted to know is if the day of fasting was finally over since the Temple was being built. In two more years, it would be completed.

In the Law, God only required one national fast. It was on the annual Day of Atonement. However, during the exile, the Jewish people instituted four additional fasts to commemorate various events.

They became "man-made" religious obligations.

- One was for a day of fasting and mourning for the capture of Jerusalem.
- Another was for the burning of the city of Jerusalem and the destruction of Solomon's Temple.
- They also remembered the day the siege began by Nebuchadnezzar against Jerusalem
- They remembered the day their governor Gedaliah was assassinated along with 80 men.

After seventy years of keeping these fasts, they wanted to know if it was time to stop the fasts. Had they fulfilled their religious obligation?

# Zechariah 7

## Just doing religious activities does not make us right with God (7:1-7)

¹"In the fourth year of King Darius, the word of the Lord came to Zechariah on the fourth day of the ninth month, which is Chislev. ² Now the town of Bethel had sent Sharezer and Regemmelech and their men to seek the favor of the Lord, ³ speaking to the priests who belong to the house of the Lord of hosts, and to the prophets, saying, "Shall I weep in the fifth month and abstain, as I have done these many years?" ⁴ Then the word of the Lord of hosts came to me, saying, ⁵ "Say to all the people of the land and to the priests, 'When you fasted and mourned in the fifth and seventh months these seventy years, was it actually for Me that you fasted? ⁶ When you eat and drink, do you not eat for yourselves and do you not drink for yourselves? ⁷ Are not these the words which the Lord proclaimed by the former prophets, when Jerusalem was inhabited and prosperous along with its cities around it, and the Negev and the foothills were inhabited?'"

### GOD ASKED THE PEOPLE THREE QUESTIONS:

**Question #1**- Did you really fast for Me? Are you genuinely sorry that the Temple, the symbol of God's presence, was destroyed, or are you sad because "things just simply aren't what they used to be?"

**Question #2**- Do you not eat & drink to yourself? - This question points to the opposite of fasting. They were feasting!

**Question #3**– Don't you understand if you had obeyed the prophets of the past all along, none of this would be happening?

His point was why do you bother remembering these events if you don't remember why they happened in the first place? Why mourn the Temple destruction when you have forgotten Me? Is it all just about religion and feeling good or is it truly obeying Me? Why are you mourning the death of Gedaliah when you have forgotten that the majority of the kings of Israel and Judah were evil and led the people into idolatry? You should be repenting instead of feasting. Four days of fasting does not make up for selfish living the rest of the year.

# Heart checkup, remember why the exile happened (7:8-14)

8 "Then the word of the Lord came to Zechariah saying, 9 "Thus has the Lord of hosts said, 'Dispense true justice and practice kindness and compassion each to his brother; 10 and do not oppress the widow or the orphan, the stranger or the poor; and do not devise evil in your hearts against one another.' 11 But they refused to pay attention and turned a stubborn shoulder and stopped their ears from hearing. 12 They made their hearts *like* flint so that they could not hear the law and the words which the Lord of hosts had sent by His Spirit through the former prophets; therefore, great wrath came from the Lord of hosts. 13 And just as He called and they would not listen, so they called and I would not listen," says the Lord of hosts; 14 "but I scattered them with a storm wind among all the nations whom they have not known. Thus, the land is desolated behind them so that no one went back and forth, for they made the pleasant land desolate."

When the heart is wrong the rituals are useless. This is not a new message. It can be found throughout the prophets and the words of Jesus in the New Testament. Israel tended to wander from God and gravitate to human works and religious rituals throughout their lives. When the prophets warned them to return to God, they were often killed by their own people. Actually, Zechariah himself would be murdered by his own people.

God reminded them that He called to His people but they wouldn't listen, so when they called in the midst of their distress, He didn't listen. We do reap what we sow. They came to ask if some of their fasts could be removed and what they got was a sharp rebuke and a history lesson about why all their troubles came in the first place.

> **Jesus speaking:**
> **"Jerusalem, Jerusalem, who kills the prophets and stones those who are sent to her! How often I wanted to gather your children together, the way a hen gathers her chicks under her wings, and you were unwilling."**
> (Matthew 23:37)
>
> **Isaiah speaking:**
> **"I hate your new moon festivals and your appointed feasts, They have become a burden to Me;
> I am weary of bearing them. So when you spread out your hands in prayer, I will hide My eyes from you;
> Yes, even though you multiply prayers, I will not listen.
> Your hands are covered with blood."** (Isaiah 1:14. 15)

God reminded the people again of the reasons they went into captivity and why the land was not producing fruit. The blessing of God had stopped. He listed several of their sins.

- They had hearts like stone, like flint, and they lacked compassion for human suffering.

- They no longer treated others with justice. Corruption ruled their courts.
- They did not treat the widows, orphans, or strangers with kindness. It was more serious than just a lack of hospitality; their hearts were cold.
- They occupied their time devising evil against each other.
- Their hearts had turned against the Law and they rejected His Word sent through the Prophets. This was dramatically demonstrated later when they murdered Zechariah on the Temple grounds.
- They stopped their ears from hearing from God, refusing correction from the Word of God. They shrugged ("turned") their shoulders.

**"Israel had turned a stubborn shoulder, like an animal that stiffened every muscle in its effort to refuse the yoke."** (Baldwin)

God reminded them "*. . . I scattered them with a storm wind among all the nations whom they have not known. Thus, the land is desolated behind them so that no one went back and forth, for they made the pleasant land desolate.*" There are additional offenses listed in other Scriptures which added to the wrath of God against His disobedient people.

Now, they had sent a delegation to Zechariah asking if they can stop four days of fasting so they can feast more. To say that God was upset with the people is an understatement. They needed a major heart exam. Are we all that different? We can act very religious and fail at the basics of godly living that are listed in these verses. It is easy to substitute religion for a true relationship with God.

Therefore, God reminded them that He "*scattered them like a whirlwind.*"

> **"I scattered them with a whirlwind: 'This refers to the swift victories and cruel conduct of the Chaldeans towards the Jews; they came upon them like a *whirlwind*; they were tossed to and fro, and up and down, everywhere scattered and confounded.'"** (Clarke)

What a reminder to us today that we need to be close and obedient to God. He will discipline his children. Proverbs 3:11 warns, "*My son, do not reject the discipline of the Lord or loathe His reproof.*"

# Zechariah 8

## Peace and Prosperity are coming to Zion (8:1-8)

¹"Then the word of the Lord of hosts came, saying, ² "Thus says the Lord of hosts, 'I am exceedingly jealous for Zion, yes, with great wrath I am jealous for her.' ³ Thus says the Lord, 'I will return to Zion and will dwell in the midst of Jerusalem. Then Jerusalem will be called the City of Truth, and the mountain of the Lord of hosts will be called the Holy Mountain.' ⁴ Thus says the Lord of hosts, 'Old men and old women will again sit in the streets of Jerusalem, each man with his staff in his hand because of age. ⁵ And the streets of the city will be filled with boys and girls playing in its streets.' ⁶ Thus says the Lord of hosts, 'If it is too difficult in the sight of the remnant of this people in those days, will it also be too difficult in My sight?' declares the Lord of hosts. ⁷ Thus says the Lord of hosts, 'Behold, I am

going to save My people from the land of the east and from the land of the west; [8] and I will bring them back and they will live in the midst of Jerusalem; and they shall be My people, and I will be their God in truth and righteousness.'"

If you lived in a city, or country, or even during a time when life was hard, this would be welcome news. Some may go through a great famine or a time of war where destruction and death are all around. However, if they had an absolute assurance that the trial was only temporary and they knew things were going to get better, that would change everything.

In Zechariah's time, Jerusalem's walls were ruined and the city was unsafe. Nobody felt safe. They had already been invaded and destroyed and now they had no protection. These verses paint a very different picture of a land and a time when safety and security will be the norm. It was a preview of the coming attraction.

Have you ever seen an advertisement for a new residential development? You probably saw children playing in a new, clean park, the tree-lined streets were not crowded, and colors were almost imaginary. It looked like heaven on earth. God referred to this type of scene when He described what the future would be like. He even reminded them, *"If it is too difficult in the sight of the remnant of this people in those days, will it also be too difficult in My sight?"* (8:6).

The people were already back from captivity when these words were spoken. God was saying a new world was coming and when God says it, it will happen. Peace and safety will be real. The scattered tribes will come home and want to return to this new hope. This promise was offered to a special group called the "Remnant." The nation overall abandoned the Lord and went after false gods but there remained a group of faithful believers in Israel that stayed true to God. For them, the promises were well worth the persecution and the wait. Listen to the future promises God described in this passage.

- God will be in the new land and dwell with His people.
- Jerusalem will be the capital city of God's government.
- Truth will be the supporting column of the new city.
- Children will grow old in a peaceful land.
- The streets will be filled with the sound of children playing without fear.
- Nothing is too difficult for God to do in order to bless His faithful people.
- God will bring all His scattered people from the remote regions of the world to live in righteousness with their King. It will be a spiritual return, not just geographical.
- Fasts will be turned into feasts.

It is likely this is a description of the millennial reign of Christ on earth. It is likely this passage is referring to the new heaven and earth since we won't grow old. Israel has never seen anything like this in history. Nobody has. God reminded them it will not be too difficult for Him to accomplish.

By the way, if you were reading this description God gave us of a place of peace and beauty, a place where happy children play in the streets with no fear and you were thinking, "I would like to live in a place like that," you do not need to give up hope. Remember, this is not just for believing Israel but for all who have put their faith in Christ. All believing Jews and believing Gentiles will be there.

# God encouraged Israel to remain strong (8:9-13)

[9] "Thus says the Lord of hosts, 'Let your hands be strong, you who are listening in these days to these words from the mouth of the prophets, *those* who *spoke* in the day that the foundation of the house of the Lord of hosts was laid, to the end that the temple might be built. [10] For before those days there was no wage for man or any wage for animal; and for him who went out or came in there was no peace because of his enemies, and I set all men one against another. [11] But now I will not treat the remnant of this people as in the former days,' declares the Lord of hosts. [12] 'For *there will be* peace for the seed: the vine will yield its fruit, the land will yield its produce and the heavens will give their dew; and I will cause the remnant of this people to inherit all these *things*. [13] It will come about that just as you were a curse among the nations, O house of Judah and house of Israel, so I will save you that you may become a blessing. Do not fear; let your hands be strong.'"

The promised blessings continue. God reminded Israel that He brought judgment on the people in the past but that time was ending. The curse on the land would end, the seed would sprout again without being disturbed or uprooted. These would have been welcomed words because the land was still barren when this promise was given. Fruit trees would be returning along with life-giving rains which had been withheld for so long. The prophet Haggai had just told them the same promise, that seeds would again be growing.

> "Do consider from this day onward, from the twenty-fourth day of the ninth month; from the day when the temple of the Lord was founded, consider: 'Is the seed still in the barn? Even including the vine, the fig tree, the

**pomegranate and the olive tree, it has not borne fruit. Yet from this day on I will bless you.'"** (Haggai 2:18, 19)

The word to the faithful was to not give up. They were to keep their hands strong and listen to the words of God through His prophets. The people that had become a curse would be a blessing to the world. The time of affliction that God allowed for a time would change to prosperity and peace. They were encouraged to trust God.

## APPLICATION

Christians can go through seasons of discouragement. Maybe we brought it on ourselves by sin or dumb decisions. Maybe it was an injury or debilitating disease. Whatever the reason, we can find ourselves at times in days of darkness and frustration. It is then that the enemy of our souls tells us we have been abandoned by God. In this passage, the root of the problems Israel faced was their sin. And yet, even when they were in a prodigal state, God never stopped loving them. He, time after time, sent messages of hope to them. They needed to get out of the dark pit, trust God again and He would guide them home. Never forget, No matter what pit we find ourselves in, God is deeper and He has amazing plans for us.

# God's plan is to bless Israel (8:14-17)

¹⁴ "For thus says the LORD OF HOSTS, 'JUST AS I PURPOSED TO DO HARM TO YOU WHEN YOUR FATHERS PROVOKED ME TO WRATH,' SAYS THE LORD OF HOSTS, 'AND I HAVE NOT RELENTED, ¹⁵ so I have again purposed in these days to do good to Jerusalem and to the house of Judah. Do not fear! ¹⁶ These are the things which you should do: speak the truth to one another; judge with truth and judgment for peace in your gates. ¹⁷ Also let none of you devise evil in your heart

against another, and do not love perjury; for all these are what I hate,' declares the LORD."

> "Israel's forefathers had been cursed because of the sins of rebellion they had committed against the Lord. They had been warned, and then they had been judged. They had been carried off to Babylon as God poured out His wrath on them. But now they have returned from that captivity. They have turned to seek the Lord, and God will once again be blessing the nation. However, they must not repeat the sins of their fathers. They must be truthful, for God hates lies and treachery."
>
> (Enduring Word Ministries)

God was saying His purposes are what will take place. When Israel disobeyed, He purposed to bring them to ruin to drive them to repentance and back to Himself. The people had returned to the land, also part of His plan. He told them He purposed to do good to them. They needed to purpose in their hearts to be truthful and honest. They needed to renounce the evil ways that had angered God. Then His purpose for good would come about.

> "'For I know the plans I have for you,' declares the Lord, 'plans to prosper you and not to harm you, plans to give you hope and a future. Then you will call on me and come and pray to me, and I will listen to you. You will seek me and find me when you seek me with all your heart.'"
>
> (Jeremiah 29:11-13)

# Fasting will become feasting (8:18-19)

18 "Then the word of the Lord of hosts came to me, saying, 19 "Thus says the Lord of hosts, 'The fast of the fourth, the fast of the fifth, the fast of the seventh and the fast of the tenth months will become joy, gladness, and cheerful feasts for the house of Judah; so love truth and peace.'"

The time for fasting was over. Remember, God had given Israel seven feasts (Leviticus 23) but only one required a fast on the annual Day of Atonement. The Jews added the other four and used them to commemorate events of their choosing. They then used those to make themselves look religious but their hearts remained far from God. Now, it was time to return to God's system. The Temple was being rebuilt and everything would get back on track. Mourning was over, there was much to celebrate.

> "None of these things had been in the purpose of God for His people; they had resulted from their sins. The fasts, therefore, were the result of their sins."
>
> (G. Campbell Morgan)

Even something as good as fasting for the right purposes had been twisted to become a system of false religion. Like the monks that live in seclusion and beat their bodies as signs of suffering for God, so Israel had developed their own system of suffering for God to make amends for their failures. They developed four different fast seasons to commemorate events of their past but made them compulsory, a test of their spirituality. Zechariah told them to stop the unofficial fasts, which had degraded into man-made feasts, and return to God's system. It was time to stop playing religion and return to a relationship with God. Then the fasting seasons would become feasting celebrations.

# The future blessing of Israel will be known by all peoples (8:20-23)

20 "Thus says the LORD OF HOSTS, '*It will* yet *be* that peoples will come, even the inhabitants of many cities. 21 The inhabitants of one will go to another, saying, "Let us go at once to entreat the favor of the LORD, AND TO SEEK THE

LORD OF HOSTS; I WILL ALSO GO." ²² So many peoples and mighty nations will come to seek the LORD OF HOSTS IN JERUSALEM AND TO ENTREAT THE FAVOR OF THE LORD.' ²³ Thus says the LORD OF HOSTS, 'IN THOSE DAYS TEN MEN FROM ALL THE NATIONS WILL GRASP THE GARMENT OF A JEW, SAYING, "LET US GO WITH YOU, FOR WE HAVE HEARD THAT GOD IS WITH YOU."'"

Again, God used the term *"in those days"* which pointed to a future day. A great day was coming for the faithful of Israel. All the abuse, persecutions, and hatred would come to an end and they would be vindicated. After the long night, the light was coming that would expose the evil done against Israel. In Christ's Millennial Kingdom the nations will recognize God as the God of Jacob. Jerusalem will be the governmental seat in that kingdom and the Law of God will come from the Lord Himself. It will be the fulfillment of what Isaiah prophesied:

> "Now it will come about that in the last days, the mountain of the house of the LORD will be established as the chief of the mountains, and will be raised above the hills; And all the nations will stream to it. And many peoples will come and say, come, let us go up to the mountain of the LORD, to the house of the God of Jacob; That He may teach us concerning His ways, and that we may walk in His paths. For the law will go forth from Zion, and the word of the LORD from Jerusalem." (Isaiah 2:2, 3)

Instead of being a despised people, the Jews will be the desired people. The nations will realize that God is with the ones He has called the "apple of His eye." The nations will want to be friends of the Jews instead of their enemies.

> "Thus says the LORD OF HOSTS, 'IN THOSE DAYS TEN MEN FROM ALL THE NATIONS WILL GRASP THE GARMENT OF A JEW, SAYING, "LET US GO WITH YOU, FOR WE HAVE HEARD THAT GOD IS WITH YOU."'" (8:23)

For the past seventy years, the Jews had a burned down city and endured the mockery of the nations. Zechariah rekindled their hope that a glorious city would be coming and they needed to be a part of that great day through faith. One day the nations will no longer despise the Jew but will want to be with them because the blessing of God will be with them. *"All the nations will grasp the garment of a Jew"* is the people saying "I want to be with you since God is with you."

> **"This prophecy teaches, then, that Israel will be the means of drawing the nations of the earth to the Lord in the time of the Messiah's reign of righteousness upon the earth."** (Feinberg)

# Section Three
## ZECHARIAH'S TWO ORACLES, PROPHETIC PROCLAMATIONS.
## (CHAPTERS 9-14)

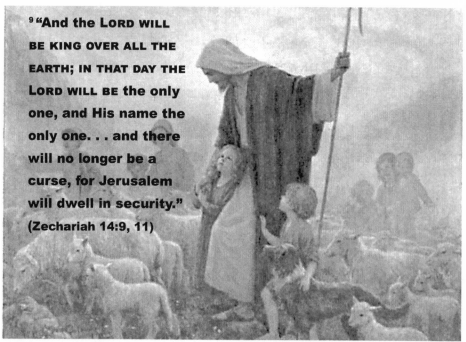

⁹ "And the LORD WILL BE KING OVER ALL THE EARTH; IN THAT DAY THE LORD WILL BE the only one, and His name the only one. . . and there will no longer be a curse, for Jerusalem will dwell in security." (Zechariah 14:9, 11)

# General Introduction
## The final section of the book of Zechariah, Chapters 9-14

Chapters 9-14 contain the largest number of Messianic prophecies found in all the minor prophets. They have similarities to the prophet Isaiah. Zechariah spoke of the Messiah, His earthly ministry and also of His second coming. Christ is pictured in both His primary roles, Savior and King. In many ways, Zechariah is a <u>major</u> minor prophet. He is unique in style and breadth of his messages when compared to the other 11 minor prophets. This uniqueness is seen most clearly in his two oracles in chapters 9-14.

**The general themes of Chapters 9 through 14**

1. The judgment of the nations who opposed Israel.
2. The protection and salvation of Israel.
3. The prophecies concerning the coming Messiah as Savior and King.

**The first oracle (9:1-11:17)** deals with Israel's rejection of the Messiah. The prophetic portions cover a time sequence that takes the reader from Zechariah's ministry in 600 B.C. to the conquests of Alexander the Great in 300 B.C. and then onto the first century Roman occupation and ministry of the Messiah, Jesus. The first oracle ends with the destruction of the Temple in 70 A.D. by Rome.

**The second oracle (12:1-14:21)**, deals with the end times when Israel will return to their King who will reign forever. The time sequence of the second oracle picks up at the battle of Armageddon and the millennial reign of Christ.

**The next page lists the Messianic prophecies found in the two oracles and their New Testament fulfillment:**

## (Charts by John Mark Hicks)

### Zechariah 9-14 and the Story of Jesus (Messianic Prophecies)

| Topic | Zechariah Text | New Testament Text |
|---|---|---|
| Royal Donkey Ride | Zechariah 9:9 | Matthew 21:5; Mark 11:1-11; John 12:15 |
| Covenant Renewal and Peace among the Nations | Zechariah 9:10-11 | Mark 14:24; Matthew 26:28 |
| The Appearance of the Lord to Deliver His People | Zechariah 9:14 | Matthew 24:31 |
| Sheep without a Good Shepherd | Zechariah 10:2 | Matthew 9:36; Mark 6:34 |
| Shepherd Rejected | Zechariah11:4-17 | Matthew 27:51-53: Mark 12:1-12 |
| Handed over to Rulers | Zechariah 11:4 | Mark 9:31 |
| Thirty Pieces of Silver: Messiah Betrayed | Zechariah 11:12-13 | Matthew 27:9-10 |
| They Will See the Pierced One: Death of the Messiah | Zechariah 12:10 | John 19:37; Matthew 26:64; Luke 21:27; Mark 14:62 |
| Mourning the Pierced One | Zechariah 12:10,14 | Luke 23:27 |
| Strike the Shepherd | Zechariah 13:7 | Matthew 26:31; Mark 14:27 |
| Fleeing of the Disciples | Zechariah 13:7 | John 16:32 |
| Shepherd Giving Life | Zechariah 13:7-9 | John 10:11, 15, 17 |
| Cleansing of the People | Zechariah 13:1,8-19 | John 7:38; Mark 14:24 |
| Cleansing Fountain | Zechariah 13:1 | John 19:43 |
| Judgment upon Jerusalem | Zechariah 14:1-2 | Matthew 24: Mark 13 |
| Behold the King | Zechariah 14:4 | Mark 11:1-12; 13:1-3 |
| All the Holy Ones with Him | Zechariah 14:5 | Matthew 24:30 |
| Moving Mountains | Zechariah 14:4 | Matthew 17:20; Mark 14:23 |
| Earthquake | Zechariah 14:3-5 | Matthew 27:51-53 |
| Living Water | Zechariah 14:8,16-19 | John 4:10; 7:38 |
| No Traders in the Temple | Zechariah 14:21 | Mark 11:15-16 |

### Zechariah 9-14 and Revelation

| Topic | Zechariah Text | New Testament Text |
|---|---|---|
| Seeing the Pierced One | Zechariah 12:10-14 | Revelation 1:7 |
| No Night There | Zechariah 14:6-7 | Revelation 21:25; 22:5 |
| Living Water in Jerusalem | Zechariah 14:8 | Revelation 22:1 |
| Jerusalem Inhabited - Never to be Destroyed | Zechariah 14:11 | Revelation 22:3 |
| Removal of the Curse | Zechariah 14:11 | Revelation 22:3 |
| Healing of the Nations | Zechariah 14:16 | Revelation 22: 2 |
| Name Inscribed | Zechariah 14:19-20 | Revelation 22:4 |
| Jerusalem is Holy | Zechariah 14:19-20 | Revelation 21:10 |
| Nothing Impure in City | Zechariah 14:21 | Revelation 21:27 |

# Zechariah chapter9
## Zechariah's first of two oracles
### COMING JUDGMENT AGAINST THE ENEMY NATIONS AND PROTECTION OF ISRAEL.

## Judgment against Lebanon (Phoenicia) (9:1-4)

[1]"The burden of the word of the Lord is against the land of Hadrach, with Damascus as its resting place (for the eyes of men, especially of all the tribes of Israel, are toward the Lord), [2] And Hamath also, which borders on it;
Tyre and Sidon, though they are very wise.
[3] For Tyre built herself a fortress
And piled up silver like dust,
And gold like the mire of the streets.
[4] Behold, the Lord will dispossess her
And cast her wealth into the sea;
And she will be consumed with fire."

This is a fascinating prophecy. The northern coastal cities of Lebanon listed in Zechariah 9:1-8 exactly describe the march of Alexander the Great's military campaign in 332-331 B.C. History shows that the prophecies against the nations given by Zechariah were fulfilled 300 years after they were given, not during Zechariah's lifetime. God has used many pagan nations to accomplish His purposes including Babylon and Greece. The destruction of Tyre's strongly fortified city, described in detail in verse three, happened exactly as predicted. Alexander the Great conquered it in seven months, something the Assyrians could not do in five years, nor the Babylonians in 13 years. God used Alexander as His instrument to execute judgment on the enemies of Israel in the cities of Lebanon.

## A LESSON WE LEARN FROM TYRE

One practical application stands out in the description of Tyre. The arrogance of the city was apparent. They had great storehouses of wealth. Their silver and gold were abundant like dust. They were attacked previously by the greatest empires yet they were not conquered. They had built such a fortified city no one could touch them. They trusted in their wealth and reputation. Tyre, they thought, was too important, too smart, too well-positioned, too wealthy to fall.

We remember the ill-fated Titanic that claimed: "Not even God could sink this ship!" We remember the rich fool Jesus talked about who felt overconfident in his riches and complimented himself on his worldly success but that very night his soul was required of him. His secure life failed him. The Titanic sank to the bottom of the Atlantic Ocean, and Tyre, like all the others who walked in pride, was destroyed by Alexander the Great. All its wealth and security were tossed into the sea. God resists the proud and gives grace to the humble. When a man thinks he stands, he will fall. Tyre hated and fought against the people of God and those who do that declare war on God Himself, which always leads to destruction.

# Judgment against the Philistine cities (9:5-8)

5 "**Ashkelon** will see *it* and be afraid.
**Gaza** too will writhe in great pain;
Also **Ekron**, for her expectation has been confounded.
Moreover, the king will perish from **Gaza**,

124

And **Ashkelon** will not be inhabited.
⁶ And a mongrel race will dwell in **Ashdod**,
And I will cut off the pride of the **Philistines**.
⁷ And I will remove their blood from their mouth
And their detestable things from between their teeth.
Then they also will be a remnant for our God,
And be like a clan in Judah,
And **Ekron** like a **Jebusite**.
⁸ But I will camp around My house because of an army,
Because of him who passes by and returns;
And no oppressor will pass over them anymore,
For now I have seen with My eyes."

After Alexander the Great destroyed the northern coastal cities of Lebanon, he then traveled down the coast to conquer the four southern Philistine cities of Ashkelon, Gaza, Ekron, and Ashdod in 332-331 B.C.

> **"This passage 'accurately foretells the conquest of the eastern Mediterranean coastlands by Greek armies under the command of Alexander the Great.'"** (Boice)

Verse eight really stands out at the end of the list of cities that would face the judgment of God. The next city on the list was the only one that would be protected by God. The Lord Himself would camp around this city when the invading army approached. Jerusalem was that city, the one He called *"My house."*

> **"But I will camp around My house because of an army,
> Because of him who passes by and returns;
> And no oppressor will pass over them anymore,
> For now I have seen with My eyes."** (9:8)

Zechariah told his people that the one coming would destroy Israel's enemies but not conquer Israel. God's presence would be there and prevent any harm from coming to His people. Another interesting detail in verse eight is that the army mentioned would first pass by Jerusalem, head south to Gaza and the southern region. The map below shows the historic route of Alexander's army which did exactly that. They conquered Tyre, then went south and attacked Gaza, passing by Jerusalem. Following a southern campaign, they returned to attack Jerusalem. As we will see that did not happen.

After conquering Tyre and the cities of Lebanon, He continued south passing by Jerusalem and conquered Gaza. After conquering the southern region, he then headed straight to

Jerusalem, the crown jewel of the area. Zechariah predicted this would happen:

> "But I will camp around My house because of an army,
> Because of him who passes by and returns" (9:8)

The accuracy of Zechariah's prophecy is stunning by itself, but the way God protected Jerusalem is even more amazing.

## HOW GOD PROTECTED JERUSALEM FROM BEING CONQUERED BY ALEXANDER THE GREAT:

Historically, Alexander the Great did plan to overthrow Jerusalem, but something miraculous happened. The Jews in the time of Alexander the Great feared him but also showed respect and were thankful he was eradicating their enemies. The Jewish historian Josephus describes what happened when Alexander approached Jerusalem with his armies:

> "And when he (Israel's high Priest) understood that he (Alexander) was not far from the city, he went out in procession, with the priests and the multitude of the citizens. The procession was venerable, and the manner of it different from that of other nations . . . as for Alexander, when he saw the multitude at a distance, in white garments, while the priests stood clothed with fine linen, and the high-priest in purple and scarlet clothing, with his mitre on his head having the golden plate on which the name of God was engraved, he approached by himself, and adored that name, and first saluted the high-priest. The Jews also did all together, with one voice, salute Alexander, and encompass him about." (Josephus, Antiquities of the Jews)

The full account of Josephus is too lengthy to put into this book but you are encouraged to read it *(Josephus' Antiquities 11.8.4-5).* **Here is a summary of what you will find:**

> *Alexander had a troubling dream where he saw the procession of priests and he knew God was warning him to do no harm to the land of Judah or Jerusalem. At that time Josephus recounted that God gave the high priest a dream that showed he was going to meet Alexander by going out in full priestly dress. That is what he did.*

> *Alexander did not destroy Jerusalem as he had the other cities in his conquest of the world, but even recognized and acknowledged the God of the Jews. That historical entry by Josephus also included another fascinating fact. After Alexander acknowledged the God of Israel, he worshipped in the Temple and afterward, the High Priest read the prophecy of Daniel to him and explained from Daniels prophecy the Alexander and the Greek empire would defeat Persia. From that, Alexander understood he was God's appointed instrument to defeat Persia which he then did when he left Jerusalem.*

God had warned He would destroy the enemies of Israel but would ultimately protect His people. He used a powerful Greek Empire with its terrifying leader to do both. As powerful as Alexander the Great was with his army of war horses and great warriors, there was another King, even more powerful. That King would come into Jerusalem 300 years later riding, not a majestic horse, but a donkey as we see in the next verse.

# The Humble King (9:9)

⁹ "Rejoice greatly, O daughter of Zion!
Shout *in triumph*, O daughter of Jerusalem!
Behold, your king is coming to you;
He is just and endowed with salvation,

Humble, and mounted on a donkey,
Even on a colt, the foal of a donkey."

The fulfillment of this Messianic prophecy is found in Matthew 21:5, Mark 11:1-11, and John 12:15. This is how Matthew 21 tells the story and quotes Zechariah:

> **"When they had approached Jerusalem and had come to Bethphage, at the Mount of Olives, then Jesus sent two disciples, saying to them, 'Go into the village opposite you, and immediately you will find a donkey tied there and a colt with her; untie them and bring them to Me. If anyone says anything to you, you shall say, "The Lord has need of them," and immediately he will send them.' This took place to fulfill what was spoken through the prophet:**
>
>> **"*Say to the daughter of Zion,
>> 'Behold your King is coming to you,
>> Gentle, and mounted on a donkey,
>> Even on a colt, the foal of a beast of burden.'"'*
>
> (Matthew 21:1-5)

God has used many nations and different people to accomplish His purpose but it is always God who is in control. He is King. And this King would come to bring salvation to all in the humblest fashion. He would be born in a simple stable and enter Jerusalem one day on a humble donkey.

> **"Behold, your king is coming to you;
> He is just and endowed with salvation,
> Humble, and mounted on a donkey,
> Even on a colt, the foal of a donkey." (9:9)**

He would be mocked as the King of the Jews at His crucifixion but will one day be proclaimed by heaven and earth as the King of kings and Lord of lords. Zechariah told his people to look ahead to the day when the enemies of Israel would be decisively defeated and their Messiah, the King, would come.

## The breadth and authority of the future reign of Christ (9:10)

10 "I will cut off the chariot from Ephraim
And the horse from Jerusalem;
And the bow of war will be cut off.
And He will speak peace to the nations;
And His dominion will be from sea to sea,
And from the River to the ends of the earth."

> **"The battle bow shall be cut off":** Zechariah 9:9 **belongs to the first coming of Jesus, but** Zechariah 9:10 **is associated with the Second Coming of Jesus when He comes in power and glory to reign over this earth for 1,000 years. On that day there will be an enforced righteousness, and He will no longer allow war -** Isaiah 2:4." (Guzik, Blue Letter Bible)

The future millennium, the thousand-year Kingdom reign of Christ, is described in several passages (Revelation 20:1-7, Psalm 72, Isaiah 2:2-4, Isaiah 11:4-9, Jeremiah 23:5-6, Luke 1:32-33 and 19:12-27, Matthew 5:18). It will be a time when wars will cease on the earth and peace will rule from sea to sea. The coming King will bring peace to the nations, everyone will be under His Righteous authority:

> **"The battle bow shall be cut off.**
> **He shall speak peace to the nations;**
> **His dominion shall be 'from sea to sea,**
> **And from the River to the ends of the earth.'"**
> (Zechariah 9:9)

## Peace among the nations and a new covenant (9:11)

11 "As for you also, because of the blood of *My* covenant with you, I have set your prisoners free from the waterless pit."

> **"for this is My blood of the covenant, which is poured out for many for forgiveness of sins."**
> (Matthew 26:28, see also Mark 14:24)

The freedom we have when we find forgiveness of sins is described in this verse as a person locked in a prison dungeon, hopeless, thirsty without a drink, and then set free from that waterless pit. Israel had been through years of drought and famine, removed from the blessings of God because of their sins, but a day of abundant blessings was coming. They have been described in many ways in Zechariah's prophecies. Living water was coming through the person of Christ, Israel's long-awaited Messiah.

# God will fight with His people (9:12-14)

<sup>12</sup>" Return to the stronghold, O prisoners who have the hope;
This very day I am declaring that I will restore double to you.<sup>13</sup> For I will bend Judah as My bow,
I will fill the bow with Ephraim.And I will stir up your sons, O Zion, against your sons, O Greece;
And I will make you like a warrior's sword.
<sup>14</sup> Then the LORD WILL APPEAR OVER THEM,
And His arrow will go forth like lightning;
And the Lord GOD WILL BLOW THE TRUMPET,
And will march in the storm winds of the south."

God promises for those who return to the blessings and safety of God, "the stronghold," that He will bless them two-fold.

God will direct and lead His people in victory. He will "bend Judah as His bow." God blows the battle trumpet. He is the

Commander in Chief and will bring success. God will use Judah (the Southern Kingdom) as His bow and Ephraim (the Northern Kingdom) as His arrows. The formerly divided kingdom will be united as a God-empowered military force.

As we have just seen, Greece will play a role in the plan of God. The Lord will use them to help destroy the enemies of God's people. Just like Babylon, which God used to punish His rebellious and disobedient people, was destroyed, so Greece will meet the same fate. Verse 13 indicates they will ultimately fall themselves. The rendering in the New American Standard (which we use throughout) is a little hard to understand. The following are some different Bible translations of that verse:

> **New International Version**
> **"I will bend Judah as I bend my bow and fill it with Ephraim. I will rouse your sons, Zion, against your sons, Greece, and make you like a warrior's sword."**
>
> **Contemporary English Version**
> **"I will use Judah as my bow and Israel as my arrow. I will take the people of Zion as my sword and attack the Greeks."**
>
> **New Living Translation (NLT)**
> **"Judah is my bow, and Israel is my arrow.**
> **Jerusalem is my sword, and like a warrior, I will brandish it against the Greeks."**

A common understanding of this verse is that God will supernaturally empower Israel to overcome Greek oppression in the centuries following the conquest of Alexander. The Maccabees historically did that with the pagan Greek king, Antiochus Epiphanes. He was a cruel dictator who tried to force the Jews to adopt his pagan Greek culture. Many see his life described in detail in Daniel 11:29-35. History reveals he erected a statue of Zeus and made sacrifices of pigs to it within the Temple in 168 B.C. He died a violent death during the revolt.

> **"These verses are prophetic of the military prowess of Israel, through the aid of the Lord God, and were signally fulfilled in the triumphs of the Maccabees over the Grecian rulers of Syria (B.C. 167-130)."**
> (Ellicott's commentary)

Another possibility is that this is still a future event for the final conflict leading up to the Millennial Kingdom. Unlike human arrows, God goes forth like lightning. Jesus spoke of this day in Matthew 24:31:

> **"And He will send forth His angels with a great trumpet and they will gather together His elect from the four winds, from one end of the sky to the other."**

God promised to be with His army in the battle to overcome all enemies and protect His children. Today, He is with us in the same way. The battle is the Lord's.

# God defends and saves His people for His Glory (9:15-17)

¹⁵ "The LORD OF HOSTS WILL DEFEND THEM.
And they will devour and trample on the sling stones;
And they will drink *and* be boisterous as with wine;
And they will be filled like a *sacrificial* basin,
*Drenched* like the corners of the altar.
¹⁶ And the LORD THEIR GOD WILL SAVE THEM IN THAT DAY
As the flock of His people;
For *they are as* the stones of a crown,
Sparkling in His land.
¹⁷ For what comeliness and beauty *will be* theirs!
Grain will make the young men flourish, and new wine the virgins."

The Message (a Bible paraphrase) translates these verses:

> "Then God will come into view,
>     his arrows flashing like lightning!
> Master God will blast his trumpet
>     and set out in a whirlwind.
> God-of-the-Angel-Armies will protect them—
>     all-out war,
> The war to end all wars,
>     no holds barred.
> Their God will save the day. He'll rescue them.
>     They'll become like sheep, gentle and soft,
> Or like gemstones in a crown,
>     catching all the colors of the sun.
> Then how they'll shine! shimmer! glow!
>     the young men robust, the young women lovely!"

The all-consuming future victory of God for His children will be a beautiful thing. We will be to Him like gemstones in His crown, reflecting the light of our King as a testimony to His glory. When Christ reigns, an abundance of grain and new wine, fullness, and fellowship, will mark that great day.

> "The Lord will answer and say to His people,
> 'Behold, I am going to send you grain, new wine and oil,
> And you will be satisfied in full with them;
> And I will never again make you a reproach among the
> nations.'" (Joel 2:19)

# The main lesson from chapter 9

God knows each of our enemies and will repay them according to His justice and in His time. We may feel abandoned at times, but be sure, He keeps perfect records and will balance the books at the right time. He is on our side and will deliver us.

# Zechariah 10

## Introduction

After a fascinating journey through time, we saw the campaigns of Alexander the Great and then were transported to the first century to meet a King making His appearance on a donkey. The chapter ended with the millennial reign of our Messiah and King. Now in chapter10, we see more about the blessings God has in store for Israel and the judgments coming to her enemies.

## Promised blessings on Israel (10:1)

¹"Ask rain from the Lord at the time of the spring rain—
The Lord who makes the storm clouds;
And He will give them showers of rain, vegetation in the field to each man."

For many seasons Israel had experienced great droughts. God had withheld the rain and crops as a judgment against His people. They abandoned his Word and He abandoned them to the Babylonian captivity.

> **"Therefore, because of you the sky has withheld its dew and the earth has withheld its produce. I called for a drought on the land, on the mountains, on the grain, on the new wine, on the oil, on what the ground produces, on men, on cattle, and on all the labor of your hands."**
> (Haggai 1:10, 11)

In verse one, Zechariah told the people to pray again for the Spring rains and God would answer them. The time of drought was over and days of refreshing were back. I am sure many of us can relate to the feeling that comes when a long period of hot dry weather is broken with the arrival of a cool refreshing rainfall. It is the signal of a new life for plant, animal and man.

# In the past, many in Israel had put their trust in idols. (10:2)

2 "For the teraphim speak iniquity,
And the diviners see lying visions
And tell false dreams;
They comfort in vain."

## WHAT ARE THE "TERAPHIM?"

"The ancient Hebrew word for idols here is teraphim, meaning common household idols. Diviners consulted the spirits of idols to predict the future. God warns His people that there is no real help from either idols or their representatives (they comfort in vain)." (Blue letter Bible)

**Ancient Sumerian Teraphim**

Israel had always lived around idolatry from Egypt to Canaan. God brought judgment against the gods of Egypt with the 10 plagues. God warned the desert wandering multitude in the time of Moses not to make or serve idols knowing the land they were going into was filled with them. Idolatry still crept into the camp. Some turned to worship stone and wood over God even when the prophets brought fiery proclamations against the practice.

> **"Then the cities of Judah and the inhabitants of Jerusalem will go and cry to the gods to whom they burn incense, but they surely will not save them in the time of their disaster."** (Jeremiah 11:12 )

The result of this misdirected trust is false hope. It is described in the next verses.

# Wandering sheep with no real Shepherd (10:2, 3)

"Therefore, *the people* wander like sheep,
They are afflicted, because there is no shepherd.
³ "My anger is kindled against the shepherds,
And I will punish the male goats;"

> **"When Jesus went ashore, He saw a large crowd, and He felt compassion for them because they were like sheep without a shepherd; and He began to teach them many things."** (Mark 6:34)

The anger of God was strong against the nations' shepherds, the religious leaders, who had lured Israel away from God, the true Shepherd. They were goats who led the sheep away from the sheepfold into regions of danger. This resulted in idolatry and confusion. Jeremiah spoke about that danger:

"For My people have committed two evils: They have forsaken Me, The fountain of living waters, To hew for themselves cisterns, Broken cisterns That can hold no water." (Jeremiah 2:13)

# From wandering sheep to powerful horses (10:3-5)

"For the LORD OF HOSTS HAS VISITED HIS FLOCK, THE HOUSE OF JUDAH,
And will make them like His majestic horse in battle.
4 "From them will come the cornerstone,
From them the tent peg,
From them the bow of battle,
From them every ruler, *all* of them together.
5 "They will be as mighty men,
Treading down *the enemy* in the mire of the streets in battle;
And they will fight, for the LORD *will be* with them;
And the riders on horses will be put to shame."

The first two verses describe the causes of Israel's problems. The scene then shifts to hope. Zechariah did this several times, first the issues then the solutions.

We have just considered famines and idolatry and a people wandering like lost sheep. In verses 3-5, the sheep become like majestic war horses, ready for victory in battle. The parts of a strong army are listed. They are strong tent pegs for storms, a strong bow for battle. They are a dependable and adequate defense, with good leadership, skilled and trustworthy to follow. With these items in place, they will be an army of mighty men. The presence of the Lord will be with them to put to shame their enemies who only have their own strength to help them. God's presence in the future will be supernatural.

"And I saw heaven opened, and behold, a white horse, and He who sat on it is called Faithful and True, and in righteousness He judges and wages war. His eyes are a flame of fire, and on His head are many diadems; and He has a name written on Him which no one knows except Himself. He is clothed with a robe dipped in blood, and His name is called The Word of God. And the armies which are in heaven, clothed in fine linen, white and clean, were following Him on white horses. From His mouth comes a sharp sword, so that with it He may strike down the nations, and He will rule them with a rod of iron; and He treads the wine press of the fierce wrath of God, the Almighty. And on His robe and on His thigh, He has a name written, 'KING OF KINGS, AND LORD OF LORDS.'"
(Revelation 19:11-16)

From these warriors for God, new leaders of integrity and faith will become the nation's cornerstone, the foundation in the building of a new Israel.

"Let us learn from this verse that everything cometh from the Lord of hosts, the God of providence as well as of grace. Those statesmen, who are the cornerstones of the great building of the state, must come from him. Those Christian men and women of experience, who seem to be as the cornerstones of our spiritual building, must come from him." (Charles Spurgeon)

The Lord has plans for good for His people.

"'For I know the plans that I have for you,' declares the Lord, 'plans for welfare and not for calamity to give you a future and a hope.'"
(Jeremiah 29:11)

# God's plan to strengthen Israel (10:6-8)

6 "I will strengthen the house of Judah,
And I will save the house of Joseph,
And I will bring them back,
Because I have had compassion on them;
And they will be as though I had not rejected them,
For I am the LORD THEIR GOD AND I WILL ANSWER THEM.
7 "Ephraim will be like a mighty man,
And their heart will be glad as if *from* wine;
Indeed, their children will see *it* and be glad,
Their heart will rejoice in the LORD.
8 I will whistle for them to gather them together,
For I have redeemed them;
And they will be as numerous as they were before."

This passage continues the promise that God is building something of substance. We are told it will be mighty and that redemption is at the heart. God has not given up on His people as it appeared when they were being disciplined in Babylon all those years. He purchased their freedom and has called them back. When he says "*And I will save the house of Joseph*" the Jews would understand they had been a shame to their ancestors but God was removing that shame. The same God that rescued the Hebrew children from bondage in Egypt will again be known as the God of the patriarchs, Abraham, Isaac, Jacob and even Joseph. Joseph's sons were given land in what became Israel, the Northern Kingdom. This promise is for both Judah and Joseph, the entire kingdom, North, and South. The promise continues to guarantee they will be as numerous as they once were when they walked with and trusted God.

> "I will strengthen the house of Judah,
> And I will save the house of Joseph,
> And I will bring them back,

Because I have had compassion on them;
And they will be as though I had not rejected them," (10:6)

# Israel's future hope of a great national restoration (10:9-12)

⁹ "When I scatter them among the peoples,
They will remember Me in far countries,
And they with their children will live and come back.
¹⁰ "I will bring them back from the land of Egypt
And gather them from Assyria;
And I will bring them into the land of Gilead and Lebanon
Until no *room* can be found for them.
¹¹ "And they will pass through the sea *of* distress
And He will strike the waves in the sea,
So that all the depths of the Nile will dry up;
And the pride of Assyria will be brought down
And the scepter of Egypt will depart.
¹² "And I will strengthen them in the LORD,
And in His name they will walk," declares the LORD."

Look at the **main verbs** in this section in the order they are listed.

**"Scatter, remember, bring back, gather, pass through, strengthen, walk."**

Israel has just endured the 70-year captivity but this is pointing to a larger story yet to happen. It speaks of a time when the Jews will be scattered all over, but remembered by God and brought home, gathered back as a family. They will pass through many obstacles but will be strengthened by God and walk with Him again. It will be a miraculous story. History shows us that the dispersion of the Jews happened over many years under various persecutions and wars. Babylon, Persia,

Greece, and Rome were all part of the story. But God never forgot His promises. God is a promise keeper.

In 1948 something happened that had never happened before in history. A people that had been dispersed over the entire earth for thousands of years came back to their homeland and became the same nation they were before the dispersions began. Against all odds, Israel became a nation again! It was Exodus all over again. The people all went back to the land God gave them from the beginning. And one day, for the believing remnant of His people, along with believing Gentiles, there will be even a greater homecoming in a New Jerusalem.

Zechariah had taken the people of the land in the sixth century B.C. on a grand tour. His night visions showed them the Temple was being rebuilt, the priesthood was restored, former sins were to be banished, and, God would be there to protect them. Then he answered their questions and confusions and religious practices and now he told them even though God had to discipline the Jews for their disobedience, He will again bless them, bring the rains back, cause their crops to grow and their enemies to be vanquished. One day they will live in a land of peace. Some of what they heard was for the time they were living in but other promises had to do with the near and distant future. In all cases it spelled HOPE.

Chapter11 will complete Zechariah's first major oracle. More warnings and judgments were proclaimed and several Messianic prophecies completed the first of his two oracles. Greece had a prominent, prophetic place in chapters nine and ten. In chapter11 the stage is set in the time of the Roman occupation and the first-century events.

# Zechariah 11

## A prophecy of a future judgment

**Note:** The prophecies in this chapter describe a series of conquests and losses. They are historically seen as looking ahead to the time when Israel will be conquered and subjugated during the Roman occupation. Several Messianic prophecies also place this prophecy at that time period. This oracle is given to Israel after the Babylonian captivity and return so it happened after those events. No event historically matches these descriptions before the Roman Empire. Also, the last chapterended with the invasion of Alexander the Great in the third century B.C. The next major nation after Greece would be the Romans, as seen in the great statue in Nebuchadnezzar's dream in Daniel chapter two. We will look at this section with this perspective in mind.

## The sound of wailing over the land (11:1-3)

¹"Open your doors, O Lebanon, That a fire may feed on your cedars.
² Wail, O cypress, for the cedar has fallen,
Because the glorious *trees* have been destroyed;
Wail, O oaks of Bashan,
For the impenetrable forest has come down.
³ There is a sound of the shepherds' wail,
For their glory is ruined;
There is a sound of the young lions' roar,
For the pride of the Jordan is ruined."

**"Open your doors, O Lebanon, that fire may devour your cedars: This describes the coming of destructive armies of judgment from the north, through Lebanon. The doors of Lebanon are the mountain passes between Lebanon and Israel. Boice comments on how this prophecy was fulfilled in the Roman campaign against Judea. 'These verses might have described the Babylonian invasion if they had been written earlier, but that was past history by Zechariah's time. There is nothing in the history of the people that comprehensive destruction of the land can refer to prior to the terrible destruction ordered by Vespasian and his successor Titus.'"** (Guzik)

Israel rejected their Messiah when He came. In 70 A.D., Titus under Roman orders destroyed the Great temple and took many Jews captive. The wailing was heard over the land. Zechariah used poetic words to describe the approaching horrible time. Lebanon in the North could not stop the Roman destruction. The cedars of Lebanon were described as weeping and wailing as were the oaks of Bashan. Every part of nature and nations cried out in anguish. The wail of the leaders and the shepherds could be heard over the land. This event was also prophesied in Daniel 9:25, 26:

> **"'Here is what you must understand: From the time the word goes out to rebuild Jerusalem until the coming of the Anointed Leader, there will be seven sevens. The rebuilding will take sixty-two sevens, including building streets and digging a moat. Those will be rough times. After the sixty-two sevens, the Anointed Leader will be killed—the end of him. The city and Sanctuary will be laid in ruins by the army of the newly arriving leader. The end will come in a rush, like a flood. War will rage right up to the end, desolation the order of the day."**
>
> (Daniel 9:25, 26, The Message, a Bible paraphrase)

# A stage play with a strong message (11:4-7)

⁴ "Thus says the LORD MY GOD, "PASTURE THE FLOCK *doomed* to slaughter. ⁵ Those who buy them slay them and go unpunished, and *each of* those who sell them says, 'Blessed be the LORD, FOR I HAVE BECOME RICH!' AND THEIR OWN SHEPHERDS HAVE NO PITY ON THEM. ⁶ For I will no longer have pity on the inhabitants of the land," declares the LORD; "BUT BEHOLD, I WILL CAUSE THE MEN TO FALL, EACH INTO ANOTHER'S POWER AND INTO THE POWER OF HIS KING; AND THEY WILL STRIKE THE LAND, AND I WILL NOT DELIVER *them* from their power." ⁷ So I pastured the flock *doomed* to slaughter, hence the afflicted of the flock. And I took for myself two staffs: the one I called Favor and the other I called Union; so I pastured the flock."

One of the unique teaching styles used by the prophet Ezekiel in his writings was that he acted out scenes like a mime at a street theatre. He cut his hair, built miniature castles and siege ramps in the dirt, lay on his side for a period of time, and he once knocked a hole in the side of his house while living in Babylon. He blindfolded himself and walked out, and that was after spitting out his breakfast while eating. These were ways he used to explain in dramatic visual parables what was happening to the folks back home in Israel while the exiles were living 700 miles away in the custody of the Babylonians. Go back and look at Ezekiel again and see for yourself.

Why mention this? Zechariah did the same thing in these next verses. God had him demonstrate what was happening to his flock, the exiles who returned with Zechariah. He did this by actually feeding some sheep that were about to be slaughtered. It was a living object lesson of what was coming in the future.

145

Zechariah's two staffs, commonly used by shepherds were named Favor (Grace) and Union (Unity). Even though the flock was doomed, the shepherd still led with grace and kept the unity of the flock. The disasters which would come on Israel could not be blamed on God, the Good Shepherd. This visual parable was ultimately warning the people who would again follow false shepherds.

## The sheep cause the broken covenant with the Shepherd (11:8-11)

[8] "Then I annihilated the three shepherds in one month, for my soul was impatient with them, and their soul also was weary of me. [9] Then I said, "I will not pasture you. What is to die, let it die, and what is to be annihilated, let it be annihilated; and let those who are left eat one another's flesh." [10] I took my staff Favor and cut it in pieces, to break my covenant which I had made with all the peoples. [11] So it was broken on that day, and thus the afflicted of the flock who were watching me realized that it was the word of the LORD."

It is not uncommon for Scripture to contrast evil and good, light and darkness, heaven and hell. The previous chapters looked forward to a great day of blessing but this chaptertells of great darkness the nation will go through first.

Three specific false shepherds were singled out. God lost patience with them just as they had given up on God, who should have been the True Shepherd of His people. One traditional view is that they represented the three offices of Prophets, Priests, and Kings, all of whom had become corrupt in the time of the Romans. Some think the Pharisees, Sadducees, and Herodians were the three classes of people that had led the people astray. Whether these three represent groups or it was three individuals, we may not fully know but they are brought to an end in judgment by God.

Because the false leaders had broken their covenant with God and had led the people astray, the staff called Favor was broken in pieces to show God's displeasure with those who had done this.

If you are in any way skeptical that Zechariah was describing a time other than the time of Christ, just look at the next verses.

# 30 pieces of silver, the key to dating this prophecy (11:12, 13)

12 "I said to them, "If it is good in your sight, give *me* my wages; but if not, never mind!" So they weighed out thirty *shekels* of silver as my wages. 13 Then the LORD SAID TO ME, "THROW IT TO THE POTTER, *that* magnificent price at which I was valued by them." So, I took the thirty *shekels* of silver and threw them to the potter in the house of the LORD. "

One commentary on this verse picks up a very important key to understanding the entire chapter. It dates this section of the first oracle to the time to Christ.

> "This is one of the easiest chapters in the Bible to interpret, due to the inspired Matthew having applied the central incident in the chapter to the betrayal of Jesus Christ for thirty pieces of silver by Judas Iscariot (Matthew 27:3-10). With that as the key to the whole chapter, the whole passage unravels with remarkable boldness and clarity." (James Burton Coffman)

Let's look at that New Testament fulfillment of what both Zechariah and Jeremiah predicted.

**"Then that which was spoken through Jeremiah the prophet was fulfilled: 'And they took the thirty pieces of silver, the price of the one whose price had been set by the sons of Israel; and they gave them for the Potter's Field, as the Lord directed me.'"** (Matthew 27:9-10)

Here's a thought – What if Judas had betrayed Jesus for 20 or 40 pieces of silver? Then Zechariah would have been a false prophet. There are over 300 specific and detailed prophecies in the Old Testament and all were fulfilled precisely in Christ. No mistakes. What are the odds of one person doing that? We will let a mathematician answer that question.

**"Peter Stoner, in his classic book** *Science Speaks*, **calculated the chance of any man fulfilling these prophecies, even down to the present time, to be 1 in 100,000,000,000,000,000 (10 to the 17th power)."**
(Josh McDowell)

Oh, yes, I forgot to mention something. Peter Stoner's calculations were not based on 300 prophecies but on just eight! Someone else describing the odds of one person fulfilling all the Biblical prophecies suggested it would be greater than Webster's unabridged dictionary happening from an explosion in a print shop!

Anyway, just a thought. Zechariah, 600 years before the birth of Christ, predicted the Messiah would be betrayed for 30 pieces of silver!

This amount of 30 pieces of silver was especially bad because Moses in the Old Testament said that was the value of a slave. Judas had not only sold out the Messiah but he did for the lowest value a person could be bought on the slave market.

**"If the ox gores a male or female slave, the owner shall give his or her master thirty shekels of silver, and the ox shall be stoned."** (Exodus 21:32)

This was the greatest insult a person could make against Jesus, namely, there were no lower human beings that existed. Isaiah described how the Jews looked at Jesus in these words:

**"A man of sorrows and acquainted with grief;**
**And like one from whom men hide their face**
**He was despised, and we did not esteem Him."**
(Isaiah 53:3)

You can probably guess how God will respond to such an insult against His Son. His judgment was severe. These are His words:

**"I will not pasture you. What is to die, let it die, and what is to be annihilated, let it be annihilated; and let those who are left eat one another's flesh." I took my staff Favor and cut it in pieces, to break my covenant which I had made with all the peoples."** (11:9,10)

God told them He will remove His protection and His provision, two things a shepherd does for his sheep. Instead of rescuing His flock, who had rejected Him, He will let them die the death they deserve. He even predicted a time when people would eat each other because it would get so bad. Here again, the Jewish historian Josephus confirmed that happened during Titus' overthrow of Jerusalem around 70 A.D. just as God had previously warned in Leviticus 26.

**"Yet if in spite of this you do not obey Me, but act with hostility against Me, then I will act with wrathful hostility against you, and I, even I, will punish you seven times for your sins. Further, you will eat the flesh of your sons and the flesh of your daughters you will eat."**
(Leviticus 26:27-29)

# FLAVIUS JOSEPHUS, THE WARS OF THE JEWS

*(Because of the Archaic words and usages in the works of Josephus, The author of this commentary has simplified the language and paraphrased portions. If you wish to read the original, it can easily be found online in* **The Wars of the Jews, Book VI, Chapter 3, Section 4***)*

"There was a certain woman that dwelt beyond Jordan, her name was Mary; her father was Eleazar, of the village Bethezob, of the house of Hyssop. She was a prominent woman of wealth, and had fled to Jerusalem with many from her area. She was there when the attacks came.

Most of what this woman owned had been seized upon. Most of what she treasured was stolen by evil guards including the food she had tried to hide. She was tormented every day by the city guards demanding things from her. She refused them and made them angry at her. Even then they decided not to kill her.

Mary was a selfless woman and when she found food she tried to share with others and even helped them before herself. The times during the siege grew more and more desperate. It became impossible to find food. People were starving. If she found any food, she decided her labors were better used for others, and not for herself.

It eventually became impossible for her to find any more food. She became very hungry to the point of starving. Her insides hurt all the time. She still didn't complain to others.

She had a young son, but she was unable to produce milk to feed him. She knew the situation was hopeless. The armies outside the city would starve everyone to death including her son.

She then decided on the most unnatural thing. She said, "O thou miserable infant! What am I keeping you alive for? You will either starve to death or become a slave of

Rome. The Romans are worse than starvation, either way it is not a life for you. For whom shall I preserve thee in this war, this famine, and this sedition? As to the war with the Romans, if they preserve our lives, we must be slaves. My only choice at this time is that you become food for me and I will endure the slavery and abuse.

As soon as she had said this, she slew her son, and then roasted him, and ate one half of him, and kept the other half by her concealed."

This incident, even though horrible, was not unique.

"A rampart was built around the city to seal off the hidden passages. Hunger became so intense that the citizens became insane with famine, resorting to murdering one another over food; they even practiced cannibalism. Those who perished were cast over the walls into piles of bodies that remained unburied. The scene of the Holy City was one of utter desolation."
(The siege of Jerusalem, The Christian Courier)

Sadly, Israel had been warned about this even in the time of Moses when he gave the Law. God promised to bless them beyond measure in Leviticus 26 but He also gave warnings of what would happen if they turned against Him.

Zechariah told the nation of Israel what they already knew but rejected and would yet reject. The time of God's longsuffering would end and great horror descends among His people.

The next thing Zechariah described was that God would break up the nation.

# Betrayal (11:14)

14 "Then I cut in pieces my second staff Union, to break the brotherhood between Judah and Israel."

The betrayal and rejection of Jesus was the beginning of the breaking up of the union which came to finality with the destruction of Jerusalem and the scattering of the Jewish people over the earth. Since they would not honor God in unity as a nation. He broke the national bond and scattered them abroad for a season. They remained in that condition until, as history shows, in 1948 Israel came home as one people. We saw that at the end of Zechariah chapter 10.

# The worthless shepherd (11:15-17)

15 "The LORD SAID TO ME, "TAKE AGAIN FOR YOURSELF THE EQUIPMENT OF A FOOLISH SHEPHERD. 16 For behold, I am going to raise up a shepherd in the land who will not care for the perishing, seek the scattered, heal the broken, or sustain the one standing, but will devour the flesh of the fat *sheep* and tear off their hoofs.17 "Woe to the worthless shepherd who leaves the flock!"

Jesus also warned the Jews in His time that there was great danger in following a false shepherd but the people even chose to free a convicted murderer and put Jesus to death. Listen to His warning, the very same warning Zechariah gave.

> "I am the good shepherd; the good shepherd lays down His life for the sheep. He who is a hired hand, and not a shepherd, who is not the owner of the sheep, sees the wolf coming, and leaves the sheep and flees, and the wolf snatches them and scatters them. He flees because he is a hired hand and is not concerned about the sheep. I am the good shepherd, and I know My own and My own know Me, even as the Father knows Me and I know the Father; and I lay down My life for the sheep." (John 10:11-15)

The ultimate false shepherd will come in the last days when many will be swayed by him. He will be the opposite of the

Good Shepherd. He is the Anti-Shepherd or Antichrist. Many believe the final verse in this first oracle is a reference to the ultimate false shepherd.

## The judgment against the destructive shepherd (11:17b)

"A sword will be on his arm
And on his right eye!
His arm will be totally withered
And his right eye will be blind."

God's judgment will ultimately take down the final enemy of Israel and of God Himself. The uses of eye and arm may refer to the great knowledge and power of the final world leader who hates the nation of Israel and tries to destroy her. The thief comes to kill and destroy.

This is a tough place to leave the story. But Zechariah has a second oracle for his people. And, as you will see there is much more to the story.

# Zechariah's second oracle
## Chapters 12-14

### INTRODUCTION

This final oracle transports us to the time of the last days. Nothing like it happened during Zechariah's day, nor has it happened in all of history. We normally understand these events taking place at the final global battle of Armageddon. The first oracle took us from Babylon to Greece to the Roman occupation in the time of Christ. It stops finally with the overthrow of Jerusalem by Rome and the scattering of the Jewish nation. In Zechariah's second oracle we see Christ, the coming reigning King.

> **"They are demonic spirits that perform signs, and they go out to the kings of the whole world, to gather them for the battle on the great day of God Almighty."**
> (Revelation 16:14)

> **"Then they gathered the kings together to the place that in Hebrew is called Armageddon."** (Revelation 16:16)

# Zechariah 12

## God's favor will always be upon Jerusalem (12:1-5)

[1]"The burden of the word of the LORD CONCERNING ISRAEL. *Thus* declares the LORD WHO STRETCHES OUT THE HEAVENS, LAYS THE FOUNDATION OF THE EARTH, AND FORMS THE SPIRIT OF MAN WITHIN HIM, [2] "Behold, I am going to make Jerusalem a cup that causes reeling to all the peoples around; and when the siege is against Jerusalem, it will also be against Judah. [3] It will come about in that day that I will make Jerusalem a heavy stone for all the peoples; all who lift it will be severely injured. And all the nations of the earth will be gathered against it. [4] In that day," declares the LORD, "I WILL STRIKE EVERY HORSE WITH BEWILDERMENT AND HIS RIDER WITH MADNESS. BUT I WILL WATCH OVER THE HOUSE OF JUDAH, WHILE I STRIKE EVERY HORSE OF THE PEOPLES WITH BLINDNESS. [5] Then the clans of Judah will say

in their hearts, 'A strong support for us are the inhabitants of Jerusalem through the LORD OF HOSTS, THEIR GOD.'"

Jerusalem is mentioned more times in the Bible than any other city, over 800 times. The last city in the Bible will be the New Jerusalem. God reaffirms the preeminence of the city in this chapter. Despite all the political intrigue and religious claims made by the nations, Jerusalem will always be the capital of Israel and the most significant city in the world. The first verse of this chaptergives a strong reason why this is true and will remain true. Before discussing the importance of the future of Jerusalem, Zechariah reminds his audience that the One who will accomplish this is the One and only Creator of the universe.

The declaration comes, not from a man, but from the One who, by Himself, stretched out the heavens and laid the foundations of the earth. We all exist because we were created and God put within us a spirit making us God-conscious beings and capable of understanding and faith. With that in mind, God tells His creature and creation that what He is about to do with Jerusalem is as certain as His character. When He spoke, everything came into being and in these verses, He has spoken about Jerusalem. He is worth listening to, it will all happen just as He says.

**Here are four predictions about Jerusalem:**

- Jerusalem will become a cup of drunkenness to the nations. The enemies of Israel will become like stumbling drunks, unable to function coherently in the presence of the work of God. Jerusalem will confound the unbelieving world.
- All the nations of the world will rise up against Jerusalem in a day that is coming. God will make that assault of no effect. Jerusalem will be like a huge rock that will crush all who try to remove it. They will be smashed to pieces

because they are actually fighting God.

- Invading armies will be confounded and confused. Their leaders will act like madmen.
- God will be there to protect and vindicate His people. He will fight for them. Even enemy horses, or weapons of war, will be rendered useless on that day. This is not too big a challenge for the One who created all things.

**"For the LORD has chosen Zion;**
**He has desired it for His dwelling place:"**
(Psalm 132:13)

# The destruction of all the nations that come against Jerusalem (12:6-9)

6 "In that day I will make the clans of Judah like a firepot among pieces of wood and a flaming torch among sheaves, so they will consume on the right hand and on the left all the surrounding peoples, while the inhabitants of Jerusalem again dwell on their own sites in Jerusalem. 7 The LORD ALSO WILL SAVE THE TENTS OF JUDAH FIRST, SO THAT THE GLORY OF THE HOUSE OF DAVID AND THE GLORY OF THE INHABITANTS OF JERUSALEM WILL NOT BE MAGNIFIED ABOVE JUDAH.

8 In that day the LORD WILL DEFEND THE INHABITANTS OF JERUSALEM, AND THE ONE WHO IS FEEBLE AMONG THEM IN THAT DAY WILL BE LIKE DAVID, AND THE HOUSE OF DAVID *will be* like God, like the angel of the LORD BEFORE THEM. 9 And in that day, I will set about to destroy all the nations that come against Jerusalem."

Twice in these verses, the phrase "*in that day*" indicates that it is a future event. This final battle on earth at Armageddon and the coming of Christ and millennial reign is the most probable time frame.

Even though Jerusalem is tiny in comparison to the surrounding enemy nations, they have God on their side so the coming victory is clearly a supernatural event. Remember, the first verse of this chaptermade sure the reader understood that everything coming is firmly under the control of the One who created all things.

The mighty attacking nations will become firewood for the fire of God indwelling the people of God, the clans of Judah. The Lion of the tribe of Judah will be ferociously fighting for His people (verse six). Judah will become the most honored of the people on that day. (verse seven)

Verse eight is a description of the Lord as the Good Shepherd. He not only provides for His flock but He protects His flock, especially the "feeble", the weak that cannot defend himself against the wolves, the attacking nations of the world. The nation will be so protected by God that many will see *the house of David will be like God.* Even the most powerless will fight like mighty King David. God will be acknowledged by all.

> **"I am the good shepherd; the good shepherd lays down His life for the sheep. He who is a hired hand, and not a shepherd, who is not the owner of the sheep, sees the wolf coming, and leaves the sheep and flees, and the wolf snatches them and scatters them. He flees because he is a hired hand and is not concerned about the sheep. I am the good shepherd, and I know My own and My own know Me, even as the Father knows Me and I know the Father; and I lay down My life for the sheep. I have other sheep, which are not of this fold; I must bring them also, and they will hear My voice; and they will become one flock with one shepherd. For this reason the Father loves Me, because I lay down My life so that I may take it again."**
> (John 10:11, 15, 17)

# A time of mourning in Jerusalem (12:10-14)

<sup>10</sup> "I will pour out on the house of David and on the inhabitants of Jerusalem, the Spirit of grace and of supplication, so that they will look on Me whom they have pierced; and they will mourn for Him, as one mourns for an only son, and they will weep bitterly over Him like the bitter weeping over a firstborn. <sup>11</sup> In that day there will be great mourning in Jerusalem, like the mourning of Hadadrimmon in the plain of Megiddo. <sup>12</sup> The land will mourn, every family by itself; the family of the house of David by itself and their wives by themselves; the family of the house of Nathan by itself and their wives by themselves; <sup>13</sup> the family of the house of Levi by itself and their wives by themselves; the family of the Shimeites by itself and their wives by themselves; <sup>14</sup> all the families that remain, every family by itself and their wives by themselves."

The day will come when the nation that crucified their Messiah will realize that the One pierced on the cross was pierced for them. The full gravity of the suffering and death of Christ on the cross will be understood and they will mourn greatly for what they did (verse 10). God has always had a believing remnant in Israel even when the nation was most rebellious. In this closing scene, God is demonstrating one great outpouring of grace to bring in His final sheep into the fold. This message from Zechariah would have been a message of hope to the people of Judah that God was with them and will always be with them. This is another of the many Messianic prophecies in Zechariah.

> **"Jesus said to him, 'You have said it yourself; nevertheless I tell you, hereafter you will see the Son of Man sitting at the right hand of Power, and coming on the clouds of heaven.'"** (Matthew 26:64)

> "But one of the soldiers pierced His side with a spear, and
> immediately blood and water came out. And he who has
> seen has testified, and his testimony is true; and he knows
> that he is telling the truth, so that you also may believe.
> For these things came to pass to fulfill the Scripture, 'Not a
> bone of Him shall be broken.' And again another Scripture
> says, 'They shall look on Him whom they pierced.'"
> (John 19:34-37)

> "Behold, He is coming with the clouds, and every eye will
> see Him, even those who pierced Him; and all the tribes
> of the earth will mourn over Him. So it is to be. Amen."
> (Revelation 1:7)

Verses 11-14 describe the mourning as a great national day of
sorrow, like when the godly King Josiah died in battle in a place
called Hadadrimmon, in the valley of Megiddo (Judges 20:47,
1 Kings 22:31-37, 2 Kings 23:29). This was the same place
where the final battle of Armageddon will be fought. The entire
nation mourned the loss then, but in the future, they will see
their Messiah and realize the full extent of His suffering and
their role as a nation in that event.

# Zechariah 13

## There is a cleansing fountain for God's people (13:1)

¹ "In that day a fountain will be opened for the house of
David and for the inhabitants of Jerusalem, for sin and for
impurity."

The previous chapterended with a description of what will happen in the last days and the final battle on the earth when Israel will supernaturally prevail. Then there will be great mourning when the people of God see their King face to face and are sorrowful for the way He was treated and abused by His own chosen people. It will be a time of repentance and grace for those who embrace their Messiah and King.

Chapter 13 begins with the words *"In that day . . ."* This chaptercontinues the thoughts in chapter 12 concerning that final day of reckoning for the children of Abraham. At the same time, a fountain of cleansing will be opened to remove the sins of the repentant.

Jesus once told the crowds that He was the source of that fountain:

> "Now on the last day, the great day of the feast, Jesus stood and cried out, saying, 'If anyone is thirsty, let him come to Me and drink. He who believes in Me, as the Scripture said, "From his innermost being will flow rivers of living water"' But this He spoke of the Spirit, whom those who believed in Him were to receive; for the Spirit was not yet given, because Jesus was not yet glorified."
> (John 7:37-39)

At the end of this age when a New Heaven and New Earth are created there is also a reference to a permanent fountain and eternal cleansing available that will flow from the throne of God. Zechariah did not say a well or pool of cleansing was available, but a fountain, a continuous flow of a cleansing stream. Here are two descriptions of the New Earth that is coming and the New Jerusalem:

> "Behold, the tabernacle of God is among men, and He will dwell among them, and they shall be His people, and God Himself will be among them, and He will wipe away

every tear from their eyes; and there will no longer be any death; there will no longer be any mourning, or crying, or pain; the first things have passed away." (Revelation 21:3, 4)

"Then he showed me a river of the water of life, clear as crystal, coming from the throne of God and of the Lamb, in the middle of its street. On either side of the river was the tree of life, bearing twelve kinds of fruit, yielding its fruit every month; and the leaves of the tree were for the healing of the nations." (Revelation 22:1, 2)

# All false prophets will be exposed and ashamed (13:2-6)

2 "It will come about in that day," declares the LORD OF HOSTS, "THAT I WILL CUT OFF THE NAMES OF THE IDOLS FROM THE LAND, AND THEY WILL NO LONGER BE REMEMBERED; AND I WILL ALSO REMOVE THE PROPHETS AND THE UNCLEAN SPIRIT FROM THE LAND. 3 And if anyone still prophesies, then his father and mother who gave birth to him will say to him, 'You shall not live, for you have spoken falsely in the name of the LORD'; AND HIS FATHER AND MOTHER WHO GAVE BIRTH TO HIM WILL PIERCE HIM THROUGH WHEN HE PROPHESIES. 4 Also it will come about in that day that the prophets will each be ashamed of his vision when he prophesies, and they will not put on a hairy robe in order to deceive; 5 but he will say, 'I am not a prophet; I am a tiller of the ground, for a man sold me as a slave in my youth.' 6 And one will say to him, 'What are these wounds between your arms?' Then he will say, '*Those* with which I was wounded in the house of my friends.'"

Final days of judgment are coming for all the false prophets who have misled the people. This passage describes how not only is God cleaning up the nation but even those responsible for misleading the people will be ashamed, their families will even put them to death if they don't cease from their false prophecies. Those who formerly made a financial gain from deception will admit their sins. It will be a day when God truly cleans house of all sin and deception. Jesus warned about those who are blind concerning truth, and the danger of others following them into their same ditch.

The time of deception is coming to an end when Jesus comes to reign. Truth will be on the throne. The wounds spoken of in verse six in the context of this section are wounds that are either self-inflicted or received from the false prophet's friends. Parents are also described as turning against their sons if they are false prophets. This will not be a good season to be on the wrong side of God. It will be a zero-tolerance time for false teachers.

# The Messiah to come will be cut off and the people scattered (13:7)

7 "Awake, O sword, against My Shepherd,
And against the man, My Associate,"
Declares the LORD OF HOSTS.
"Strike the Shepherd that the sheep may be scattered;
And I will turn My hand against the little ones."

This prophetic section is a reminder to Israel of what will happen when their Messiah first comes to earth. He will be cut off (crucified). After that, the nation will be scattered and ultimately a time of great tribulation will come on the whole earth. Several Messianic prophecies are included in these verses. Remember, this prophecy and others in Zechariah were given in 600 B.C. All of his prophecies then were yet to come. In our time, some have been fulfilled and others yet to be fulfilled.

162

The first prophecy in verse seven is clear that the coming of the Messiah and His appointed death is determined by the Father, not an accident. After the Last Supper meal Jesus quoted this passage from Zechariah:

> **"Then Jesus said to them, 'You will all fall away because of Me this night, for it is written, "I will strike down the shepherd, and the sheep of the flock shall be scattered." But after I have been raised, I will go ahead of you to Galilee.'"**

(Matthew 26:31, also Mark 14:27 and John 16:32)

Isaiah also referred to the coming death of the Messiah and that it was the plan of God from the beginning.

> **"He was oppressed and He was afflicted,**
> **Yet He did not open His mouth;**
> **Like a lamb that is led to slaughter,**
> **And like a sheep that is silent before its shearers,**
> **So He did not open His mouth.**
> **By oppression and judgment He was taken away;**
> **And as for His generation, who considered**
> **That He was cut off out of the land of the living**
> **For the transgression of my people, to whom**
> **the stroke was due?**
> **His grave was assigned with wicked men,**
> **Yet He was with a rich man in His death,**
> **Because He had done no violence,**
> **Nor was there any deceit in His mouth.**
> **But the Lord was pleased**
> **To crush Him, putting Him to grief"**

(Isaiah 53:7-10)

# The refining and saving of a remnant of Israel (Verses 8, 9)

[8] "It will come about in all the land,"
Declares the LORD,
"That two parts in it will be cut off *and* perish;

163

But the third will be left in it.
<sup>9</sup> "And I will bring the third part through the fire,
Refine them as silver is refined,
And test them as gold is tested.
They will call on My name,
And I will answer them;
I will say, 'They are My people,'
And they will say, 'The LORD IS MY GOD.'"

Verses eight and nine shift the scene back to the end times. It seems that it had to be established that it was the Father's will for His Son to come and be cut off and for Israel to be scattered. Even though the Great Tribulation is coming and it seems from this passage that two-thirds of Israel will perish, God will preserve one-third in that day as part of His remnant to be saved. Remember, God is eternally present in all of time; He is the great I Am. He has already seen everything that is coming and He is giving a glimpse of some of that to Israel.

After the days and years of the dispersion of Israel, a great time of trial and testing will come on Israel. Jesus warned that it would happen. It is what Jeremiah referred to as the time of Jacob's trouble.

> "Alas! for that day is great,
> There is none like it;
> And it is the time of Jacob's distress,
> But he will be saved from it. It shall come about on that day,' declares the Lord of hosts, 'that I will break his yoke from off their neck and will tear off their bonds; and strangers will no longer make them their slaves. But they shall serve the Lord their God and David their king, whom I will raise up for them." (Jeremiah 30:7, 8)

> "Therefore when you see the abomination of desolation which was spoken of through Daniel the prophet, standing in the holy place (let the reader understand), then those who are in Judea must flee to the mountains. . . .

> For then there will be a great tribulation, such as has not
> occurred since the beginning of the world until now, nor
> ever will. Unless those days had been cut short, no life
> would have been saved; but for the sake of the elect those
> days will be cut short." (Matthew 24:15, 16, 21, 22)

The elect Jesus was talking about will go through great trials
and refinement like one in a purifying furnace. They will come
out and call upon the name of the Lord. Read again
Zechariah 13:9 and the commentary that follows:

> "And I will bring the third part through the fire,
> Refine them as silver is refined,
> And test them as gold is tested.
> They will call on My name,
> And I will answer them;
> I will say, 'They are My people,'
> And they will say, 'The Lord is my God.'" (13:9)

> "Though that remnant will be refined through the fires
> of suffering, one glorious day it will call on His name. On
> that day the Jewish people will be heard by Him and once
> again be gathered into the care of their smitten but
> resurrected Shepherd to confess together, 'The LORD is
> my God.'" (13:9, Israel my Glory commentary)

# Zechariah 14
## The glorious second coming of Christ

The final chapter of Zechariah is like the icing on the cake. It
contains the most Messianic prophecies of any other chapter. No
other book in the Bible has more references to the Messiah except
for Isaiah. In some ways, Zechariah is a MAJOR minor prophet. As
we have seen by his style and varieties of content are quite unique.
He went from visons to proclamations to oracles and burdens. He
also had poetry and lamentations. He now concludes his writing

with a mountain top view of the coming Messiah, Jesus. Remember, as you read this, that he wrote 600 years before Jesus was born.

# The future siege of Jerusalem (14:1, 2)

[1]"Behold, a day is coming for the LORD WHEN THE SPOIL TAKEN FROM YOU WILL BE DIVIDED AMONG YOU. [2] For I will gather all the nations against Jerusalem to battle, and the city will be captured, the houses plundered, the women ravished and half of the city exiled, but the rest of the people will not be cut off from the city."

We have seen this same plundering of Jerusalem by the nations we have seen in previous chapters. Three Gospels tell of Jesus answering the questions about the future of the Temple and the last days before He returns. Matthew 24, Mark 13 and Luke 21 record that conversation. The main points in Zechariah 14:1, 2 are as follows:

- Jerusalem will come under a major assault. The invaders will plunder away any valuable items and people from the land.
- God will gather the nations against Jerusalem in that day and capture the city.
- Houses will be destroyed and the women will be abused by the army.
- Half of all the city will be taken into exile, others will be left behind.

Some believe these things happened in 70 A.D. when Titus destroyed the temple and the city of Jerusalem. He took slaves and many spoils of war back to Rome. It may be that was just a preview of the greater plunder that will yet come in the latter days. This verse begins with the words, *"Behold, a day is coming."* The previous chapters of Zechariah describe events that have never happened in human history up to today. They are yet to happen. Jesus said that there will be great tribulation in the latter days. We find out about that in Revelation chapters four through 19. Revelation was written 20 years after the siege of Jerusalem by Titus so these events are still future.

The conclusion is that the events of Zechariah 14, like previous chapters, are primarily about the *"day"* or times of the end, the tribulation period, the millennial reign and ultimately the New Heaven and New Earth. They are one event, one period of time when they will all happen.

One additional reason to see these events as future and not history from our perspective today are verses three and four. They are clearly connected to the previous verses and describe a future event, not one that happened in 70 A.D. Verse three, begins with the word *"Then."*

# The return of Christ to the Mount of Olives (14:3-5)

3 "Then the Lord will go forth and fight against those nations, as when He fights on a day of battle. 4 In that day His feet will stand on the Mount of Olives, which is in front of Jerusalem on the east; and the Mount of Olives will be split in its middle from east to west by a very large valley, so that half of the mountain will move toward the north and the other half toward the south." 5 "You will flee by the valley of My mountains, for the valley of the mountains will reach to Azel; yes, you will flee just as you fled before the earthquake in the days of Uzziah king of Judah. Then the Lord, my God, will come, and all the holy ones with Him!"

Verse three is not just a coming battle. It is the fury of the Lord fighting against the enemies of Israel. Isaiah describes God in a similar role:

> "The Lord goes out like a mighty man, like a man of war he stirs up his zeal; he cries out, he shouts aloud, he shows himself mighty against his foes. For a long time I have held my peace; I have kept still and restrained myself; now I will cry out like a woman in labor; I will gasp and pant. I will lay waste mountains and hills, and dry up all their vegetation; I will turn the rivers into islands, and dry up the pools." (Isaiah 42:13–15)

When Jesus ascended to Heaven, He was standing on the Mount of Olives. An angel said that Jesus would come again in the same way He left. Zechariah tells us it will be at that very spot, the Mount of Olives. When Christ returns there, the mountain will split in two forming a great valley. This seems to happen when Christ and His heavenly armies return in Revelation 19 to destroy the nations and establish His reign on the earth (Revelation 20.) Zechariah's description of the Mount of Olives is the only one in the Bible but it fits within the other narratives of the coming of Christ.

Zechariah then tells his listeners that in those days the people of God will flee through that valley that was just formed.

## THE VALLEY OF ESCAPE (14:5)

5 "You will flee by the valley of My mountains, for the valley of the mountains will reach to Azel; yes, you will flee just as you fled before the earthquake in the days of Uzziah king of Judah. Then the Lord, my God, will come, *and* all the holy ones with Him!"

They will be fleeing the coming destruction of the opposing

nations. There appears to be a parallel to something that the children of Israel knew very well. Moses stood on the banks of the Red Sea, surrounded by an invading army seeking to destroy them. With hands outstretched, God parted the sea and made a valley through the sea that the people escaped through and then God destroyed the enemy. It may be a similar scene in the last days when Israel's Great Deliverer returns.

The last part of verse five describes the Lord's return with His holy ones with Him. Revelation 19 and Matthew 24 describe the fulfillment of that prophecy.

> "And I saw heaven opened, and behold, a white horse, and He who sat on it is called Faithful and True, and in righteousness He judges and wages war. His eyes are a flame of fire, and on His head are many diadems; and He has a name written on Him which no one knows except Himself. He is clothed with a robe dipped in blood, and His name is called The Word of God. And the armies which are in heaven, clothed in fine linen, white and clean, were following Him on white horses." (Revelation 19:11-14)

> "And then the sign of the Son of Man will appear in the sky, and then all the tribes of the earth will mourn, and they will see the Son of Man coming on the clouds of the sky with power and great glory. And He will send forth His angels with a great trumpet and they will gather together His elect from the four winds, from one end of the sky to the other." (Matthew 24:30, 31)

# Messiah's Kingdom will come (14:6-8)

[6] "In that day there will be no light; the luminaries will dwindle. [7] For it will be a unique day which is known to the Lord, neither day nor night, but it will come about that at evening time there will be light." [8] "And in that day living

169

waters will flow out of Jerusalem, half of them toward the eastern sea and the other half toward the western sea; it will be in summer as well as in winter."

What an interesting time this will be! The sun and moon will not give their light. This sounds like the great day Jesus talked about at the end of the tribulation when the New Jerusalem will not have darkness anymore and Christ will be the light of the eternal City. First, here is what Jesus told His disciples about the times of the end:

> "But immediately after the tribulation of those days the sun will be darkened, and the moon will not give its light, and the stars will fall from the sky, and the powers of the heavens will be shaken." (Matthew 24:29)

Now, here is how Revelation describes the Heavenly City and the New Jerusalem:

> "I saw no temple in it, for the Lord God the Almighty and the Lamb are its temple. And the city has no need of the sun or of the moon to shine on it, for the glory of God has illumined it, and its lamp is the Lamb. The nations will walk by its light, and the kings of the earth will bring their glory into it." (Revelation 21:22-24)

## LIVING WATERS (14:8)

> "And in that day living waters will flow out of Jerusalem, half of them toward the eastern sea and the other half toward the western sea; it will be in summer as well as in winter." (Zechariah 14:8)

Since this entire scene is about the time when the enemies of Israel are defeated and Christ returns and reigns for a thousand years, most commentators view the "living waters" as a symbolic picture of the truth of Christ that flows over the earth. Those living then will be with the source of living water Himself (John 4:10; 7:38) on a perfect new world, where there will always be light; no darkness at all. When the millennial reign of Christ is complete and the last judgments are complete, there will be a new heaven and new earth. It is interesting that in this eternal state there is another picture of "living waters" flowing out from God's throne.

> **"Then the angel showed me the river of the water of life, as clear as crystal, flowing from the throne of God and of the Lamb down the middle of the great street of the city."**
> (Revelation 22:1, 2)

# The Kingdom of our Messiah, a place of safety, no more curse. God is King. (14:9-11)

9 "And the LORD WILL BE KING OVER ALL THE EARTH; IN THAT DAY THE LORD WILL BE *the only* one, and His name *the only* one.

10 All the land will be changed into a plain from Geba to Rimmon south of Jerusalem; but Jerusalem will rise and remain on its site from Benjamin's Gate as far as the place of the First Gate to the Corner Gate, and from the Tower of Hananel to the king's wine presses. 11 People will live in it, and there will no longer be a curse, for Jerusalem will dwell in security."

Zechariah painted a beautiful image of hope for all of his people who truly had faith. No matter what they had been through and no matter what challenges lay ahead, the end of the story is amazing for all of God's true children. This hope is for all of God's people, Jew and Gentile alike. Gentile believers are grafted into the root of the olive tree (Romans 11). Together with the remnant of Israel, they are one in the Kingdom of God and joint-heirs of the promises of God.

Zechariah tells of a day when there will be no more curse. The earth has never been free of the curse since the fall of man when God cursed the man, the woman, the serpent and the ground. Romans eight is clear that the curse on the ground included the entire universe.

> **"For the anxious longing of the creation waits eagerly for the revealing of the sons of God. For the creation was subjected to futility, not willingly, but because of Him who subjected it, in hope that the creation itself also will be set free from its slavery to corruption into the freedom of the glory of the children of God. For we know that the whole creation groans and suffers the pains of childbirth together until now."** (Romans 8:19, 22)

When will that day come that the creation will be set free from the curse? The final answer comes when God creates a New Heaven and a New Earth. What a day that will be, a day that never ends.

> **"There will no longer be any curse; and the throne of God and of the Lamb will be in it, and His bond-servants will serve Him; they will see His face, and His name will be on their foreheads. And there will no longer be any night; and they will not have need of the light of a lamp nor the light of the sun, because the Lord God will illumine them; and they will reign forever and ever."** (Revelation 22:3-5)

For the enemies of Israel, Zechariah completes his work with a series of warnings and judgments that will be coming. The coming of the Messiah the first time was in a humble shelter in a manger but He is coming this next time in great power and glory. Paul wrote about this second coming to the church in Thessalonica:

> "... the Lord Jesus will be revealed from heaven with His mighty angels in flaming fire, dealing out retribution to those who do not know God and to those who do not obey the gospel of our Lord Jesus. These will pay the penalty of eternal destruction, away from the presence of the Lord and from the glory of His power." (2 Thessalonians 1:8, 9)

# Coming plagues for the enemies of Israel (14:12-15)

12 "Now this will be the plague with which the LORD WILL STRIKE ALL THE PEOPLES WHO HAVE GONE TO WAR AGAINST JERUSALEM; THEIR FLESH WILL ROT WHILE THEY STAND ON THEIR FEET, AND THEIR EYES WILL ROT IN THEIR SOCKETS, AND THEIR TONGUE WILL ROT IN THEIR MOUTH. 13 It will come about in that day that a great panic from the LORD WILL FALL ON THEM; AND THEY WILL SEIZE ONE ANOTHER'S HAND, AND THE HAND OF ONE WILL BE LIFTED AGAINST THE HAND OF ANOTHER. 14 Judah also will fight at Jerusalem; and the wealth of all the surrounding nations will be gathered, gold and silver and garments in great abundance. 15 So also like this plague will be the plague on the horse, the mule, the camel, the donkey and all the cattle that will be in those camps."

The awesome description in Revelation of the coming of Christ in the clouds with His mighty army may explain verse 12. Jesus' eyes are described in Revelation as *"flames of fire,"* His robe is *"dipped in blood,"* He *"strikes down the nations,"* and He treads the winepress of the fierce wrath of God, the Almighty. These descriptions of Jesus, the mighty God, are of a warrior dealing out retribution against all who know not God. His wrathful presence may be what melts the eyes of His enemies in their sockets.

> "And I saw heaven opened, and behold, a white horse, and He who sat on it is called Faithful and True, and in righteousness He judges and wages war. His eyes are a flame of fire, and on His head are many diadems; and He has a name written on Him which no one knows except Himself. 13 He is clothed with a robe dipped in blood, and His name is called The Word of God. And the armies which are in heaven, clothed in fine linen, white and clean, were following Him on white horses. From His mouth comes a sharp sword, so that with it He may strike down the nations, and He will rule them with a rod of iron; and He treads the wine press of the fierce wrath of God, the Almighty. And on His robe and on His thigh He has a name written, 'KING OF KINGS, AND LORD OF LORDS.'"
> (Revelation 19:11:16)

The plague God will send on the enemies of God's people will also come upon the animals, and the people of God will gather the gold, silver and fancy garments left behind. The plunder will be complete. Following the return of Christ recorded in Revelation, chapter 20 tells of the thousand-year reign of Christ.

# The healing of the nations during Christ's earthly reign. (14:16-21)

16 "Then it will come about that any who are left of all the nations that went against Jerusalem will go up from year to year to worship the King, the LORD OF HOSTS, AND TO CELEBRATE THE FEAST OF BOOTHS.

17 And it will be that whichever of the families of the earth does not go up to Jerusalem to worship the King, the LORD

OF HOSTS, THERE WILL BE NO RAIN ON THEM. [18] If the family of Egypt does not go up or enter, then no *rain will fall* on them; it will be the plague with which the LORD SMITES THE NATIONS WHO DO NOT GO UP TO CELEBRATE THE FEAST OF BOOTHS. [19] This will be the punishment of Egypt, and the punishment of all the nations who do not go up to celebrate the Feast of Booths.

[20] In that day there will *be inscribed* on the bells of the horses, "HOLY TO THE LORD." And the cooking pots in the LORD'S HOUSE WILL BE LIKE THE BOWLS BEFORE THE ALTAR.

[21] Every cooking pot in Jerusalem and in Judah will be holy to the LORD OF HOSTS; AND ALL WHO SACRIFICE WILL COME AND TAKE OF THEM AND BOIL IN THEM. AND THERE WILL NO LONGER BE A CANAANITE IN THE HOUSE OF THE LORD OF HOSTS IN THAT DAY."

One can only wonder what the people living in Jerusalem in the sixth century B.C. thought when they heard these words. It was certainly not like anything they had ever heard or imagined. The Messiah will reign on the earth one day after he has vanquished all the enemies of Israel. The feasts and Temple will be reestablished on the earth as a memorial to the Messiah who will reign for a thousand years. Then one day there will never be a curse again and Messiah will be the light of all, no more night, or pain, or Canaanites, or sin. What thoughts must have amazed the people of Zechariah's time over 2,600 years ago? We still sit stunned today when we read these things and our own spirits cry out for that time.

**Important note:** The reestablishment of animal sacrifices in the millennial reign of Christ is not about payment for sin. It will be a memorial much like we have a communion service to remember the Lord's death. The Jews will have the Lamb of God present on the earth and the sacrifices will be seen for what they were meant to be, a shadow of the One who came and died once for all for sin. The millennial sacrifices will act as an object lesson and a time of worship for the Lamb who was slain. It was never the blood of bulls and goats that saved back then and it will not be in the future either.

The Temple has quite a history in the Bible. It was always a shadow of the cross, meant to illustrate to mankind that the way back to God for the sinner was through the shed blood of the Lamb of God. Until Jesus actually came, the people had the Temple system to follow by faith knowing that the final sacrifice was still coming. The Temple of Solomon was destroyed by Nebuchadnezzar and his army. It was later rebuilt under the leadership of Zerubbabel. That second temple was later reconstructed by King Herod in the first century. That temple was also destroyed, this time in 70 A.D. by Titus, a Roman general.

There has not been a temple in Jerusalem since that time. Many of the feasts of Israel were centered around Temple activities as was the work of the priests and High Priest. Without a Temple, the feasts and many of the Jewish practices were at best merely a shadow of the past glory that once was Israel. The glory of Israel was gone.

There is one more Temple to come. Ezekiel chapters 40-48 go into great detail describing this future Temple. What he describes has never to this day been seen on the earth. It is different from the other temples. Ezekiel's Temple will be used during the millennial reign of Christ. The feasts of Israel will be restored and believers will again travel to Jerusalem to celebrate them. (Leviticus 23).

As noted, one of the surprising practices during Christ's earthly reign will be the use of animal sacrifices (Ezekiel 43-46).

Jesus died once for all and it is finished. These sacrifices will not be for the purpose of seeking forgiveness of sins. They are a memorial, remembering the past and rejoicing in the fact that we have a living Savior. Zechariah reveals to us in this passage some details about the Millennial sacrifices to come.

> "And the cooking pots in the Lord's house will be like the bowls before the altar. Every cooking pot in Jerusalem and in Judah will be holy to the Lord of hosts; and all who sacrifice will come and take of them and boil in them." (14:20, 21)

> "The pots in the LORD's house: These were the cooking utensils used by worshippers to cook for their own the sacrificial meat intended for them from the peace offerings. The bowls before the altar were used to gather and sprinkle sacrificial blood on the altar. These show that animal sacrifice will continue in the millennium, but *not as atonement for sin* – which was perfectly satisfied by the atoning work of Jesus. Sacrifice in the millennium will look back to the perfect work of Jesus."
> (Guzik, Blue Letter Bible)

# A final note

When Christ comes and reigns, even the everyday items we use will be holy because they are part of the worship of the King. The cooking utensils, everything. In the past, the phrase, "*HOLY TO THE LORD*" was engraved on the gold crown the High Priest wore. This, of course, pointed to our Great High Priest who is by nature holy. In the Millennial reign, Christ will be present on the earth, and everything associated with Him will be holy, even the bells on the horses as this text shows. With God, nothing is common.

Don't forget, as a believer, you are not common either to God. He has set you apart for Himself and has engraved those same words on your heart, *"Holy unto the Lord."*

With that, the book of Zechariah comes to an end. There is no other book quite like it. God gave Zechariah the privilege of seeing and understanding things we wish we could see and better understand. One day we will if we know Christ.

> **"For now we see in a mirror dimly, but then face to face; now I know in part, but then I will know fully just as I also have been fully known."** (1 Corinthians 13:12)

**Amen and Amen!**

"But as it is written, what no eye has seen, nor ear heard, nor the heart of man imagined, what God has prepared for those that love Him."

1 Corinthians 2:9 ESV

# God's final messenger in the old testament

5 "Behold, I am going to send you Elijah the prophet before the coming of the great and terrible day of the LORD."

Malachi 4:5

# Introduction

## God's final messenger

We come to the final book of the Old Testament, the last voice of the prophets before a deafening period of silence fell over time like a deep fog. The people of God listened for a fresh word coming from God yet none will be heard for the next 400 years. Then, when hope was drained, God spoke again and what a voice it was. The cry, "*It is finished*" still echoes all over the earth to this day. Today we wait again for one final shout from God and it is coming with a mighty trumpet blast. We will now examine that last voice of the Old Testament era; the final instructions and warnings to carry the people through the centuries. What will God tell them through His prophet, Malachi? Let's find out.

Malachi's name means "My messenger." The prophets were, by definition, mouthpieces for God. They were how God spoke to men.

> **"God, after He spoke long ago to the fathers in the prophets in many portions and in many ways, in these last days has spoken to us in His Son, whom He appointed heir of all things, through whom also He made the world."**
> (Hebrews 1:1, 2)

The prophets were the voice of God until the day when God Himself would have the final word. He has "*spoken to us in His Son.*"

We know very little about this final prophet of the Old Testament. Maybe that is because we are usually interested only in the news messengers bring. Malachi wrote around 400 B.C. The Temple had been rebuilt, the priesthood and sacrifices reinstituted, the Law restored through Ezra, and the protective walls were around the city because of Nehemiah. It should have been a time of peace, growth and a day when God was honored for all He had done. Unfortunately, the frequently rebellious people of God were back again questioning everything God told them.

When you read Malachi, try to imagine a courtroom scene. God is both Judge and Prosecuting Attorney. The Jews are the defendants trying to argue their case. The book of Malachi is arranged in a series of seven charges by God followed by the complaints and questions by Israel. Then Malachi presents God's answers to the complaints. It is like a heated courtroom exchange. This back and forth confrontation is a unique style to the book of Malachi. Here are the questions asked by the Jewish people in response to God's charges:

- In what way have You loved us? (1:2)
- In what way have we despised Your name? (1:6)
- In what way have we defiled You? (1:7)
- In what way have we wearied You? (2:17)
- In what way shall we return? (3:7)
- In what way have we robbed You? (3:8)
- In what way have we spoken against You? (3:13)

# The big issue

At stake throughout this book is whether the Jewish people were still in a covenant relationship with God. Had they jeopardized their privileged position being the chosen people of God? Had they destroyed their place in the Abrahamic Covenant? Did they find the answers in the responses God gives to their questions?

> **"The term covenant occurs seven times in the book. References are made to "my covenant" (2:5), "the covenant with Levi" (2:8), "the covenant of our fathers" (2:10), "the marriage covenant" (2:14), and the "messenger of the covenant" (3:1). The respect and obedience to the stipulations of these covenants are most evident in the**

disputations that make up the bulk of the book."
(Charles Savelle)

"So, what is the point of Malachi? It is to answer the BIG covenantal questions on the minds of the people in Malachi's day... "Is God still our God? Are we still his people? Is His program for us still on track? Does His law still apply to us? Should we still be living as God originally called Israel to live, or have things changed? God's answer in the prophecy is... "You are still my people. I still love you. We are still in the covenant. I am keeping my end of the covenant. Now keep yours. Be my people in this generation and you will see my promises for you fulfilled. Or, put more simply — I am the Lord. I do not change."
(Think Theology)

We begin with what one would think is an unquestionable truth of God. His love for the world and His love for the children of Abraham. Who could question that, right? Welcome to the book of Malachi.

# Malachi 1
## Questions and more questions

### ISRAEL QUESTIONED IF GOD ACTUALLY LOVED THEM (1:1-5)

¹ The oracle of the word of the LORD to Israel through Malachi. ² "I have loved you," says the LORD. But you say, "How have You loved us?" "*Was* not Esau Jacob's brother?" declares the LORD. "Yet I have loved Jacob; ³ but I have hated Esau, and I have made his mountains a desolation and *appointed* his inheritance for the jackals of the wilderness." ⁴ Though Edom says, "We have been beaten down, but we will return and build up the ruins"; thus says the LORD of hosts, "They may build, but I will tear down; and *men* will call them the wicked territory, and the people

toward whom the LORD is indignant forever." [5] Your eyes will see this and you will say, "The LORD be magnified beyond the border of Israel!"

God began with a simple but wonderful and heartfelt truth, *"I have loved you."* Through the centuries the people of God had rebelled, lied, embraced false gods, served idols, married pagan nations, killed the prophets, etc. God never stopped loving them. He did what a loving father would do to a child. He disciplined when necessary, often severely. He brought words of comfort, hope and gave instruction along with warnings. He parented the headstrong people, but only because He loved them. Now, they asked God, *"How have You loved us?"*

His answer was basically telling them that they should look again at what happened to Edom. Isaac had two sons, Jacob and Esau. Malachi's audience descended from the sons of Jacob. The earlier book of Obadiah handled the judgments against Edom and the total destruction God had determined for them. God was telling the sons of Jacob in this letter, if He didn't love Israel, then they would be under the same curse as Edom. They were being blessed because they were chosen by God. The crops were back, the Temple was back, sacrifices were back. God was back. That was only because God had demonstrated His love in so many ways. The curses He was sending against their kin, Esau, were more proof of His love protecting them against their enemies.

God reminded them that even if Edom tried to rebuild, He would knock it down again. That day was yet to fully happen but God reminded them it would happen. They needed to be patient because on that day, *"Your eyes will see this and you will say, "The Lord be magnified beyond the border of Israel!"* The condemnation to Edom would extend to all generations. They would never successfully rebuild. The real comfort to Israel was not just that their enemies would be permanently destroyed. The same God that had made that promise told His children they were chosen and loved. This also applied to future generations. He would keep them in His hand and fulfill all the promises made to them with the same certainty as His judgments against Edom. He could have just as easily brought them the same judgment as Esau, *"Yet I have loved Jacob; but I have hated Esau, and I have made his mountains a desolation.*

God's answer to this first complaint is, Yes, my children, I have indeed loved you and I still do.

## ISRAEL DISRESPECTED THE NAME OF THE LORD (1:6-14)

⁶ "'A son honors *his* father, and a servant his master. Then if I am a father, where is My honor? And if I am a master, where is My respect?' says the LORD of hosts to you, O priests who despise My name. But you say, 'How have we despised Your name?' ⁷ *You* are presenting defiled food upon My altar. But you say, 'How have we defiled You?' In that you say, 'The table of the LORD is to be despised.' ⁸ But when you present the blind for sacrifice, is it not evil? And when you present the lame and sick, is it not evil? Why not offer it to your governor? Would he be pleased with you? Or would he receive you kindly?" says the LORD of hosts. ⁹ "But now will you not entreat God's favor, that He may be gracious to us? With such an offering on your part, will He receive any of you kindly?" says the LORD of hosts. ¹⁰ "Oh that there were one among you who would shut the gates, that you might not uselessly kindle *fire on* My altar! I am not pleased with you," says the LORD of hosts, "nor will I accept an offering from you. ¹¹ For from the rising of the sun even to its setting, My name *will be* great among the nations, and in every place incense is going to be offered to My name, and a

grain offering *that is* pure; for My name *will be* great among the nations," says the LORD of hosts. ¹²"But you are profaning it, in that you say, 'The table of the Lord is defiled, and as for its fruit, its food is to be despised.' ¹³ You also say, 'My, how tiresome it is!' And you disdainfully sniff at it," says the LORD of hosts, "and you bring what was taken by robbery and *what is* lame or sick; so you bring the offering! Should I receive that from your hand?" says the LORD. ¹⁴"But cursed be the swindler who has a male in his flock and vows it, but sacrifices a blemished animal to the Lord, for I am a great King," says the LORD of hosts, "and My name is feared among the nations."

The conversation then turned to how Israel had been treating God. The prophet brought two strong accusations against the Jewish nation. He reminded them that God is their Master and they had been greatly disrespecting Him. Then He added that they had actually despised the name of God. Israel challenged those charges. They asked, "How have we despised Your name?'" "*How have we defiled You*?" God then answered both of these denials. He built His case against Israel by describing how the nations had violated the sacrificial system He established.

## IN BRIEF HERE IS THE BASIS FOR THE ACCUSATIONS:

God established the entire Old Testament system of priests and sacrifices. These were the ways God communicated to man his lost condition and his need for forgiveness. All who approached God needed to come by faith with the shedding of the blood of an innocent victim, usually a lamb or other sacrificial animal.

God was very specific that the animals to be sacrificed needed to be the best and unblemished. After all, this was picturing the final sacrifice that would come one day, the unblemished Son of

God, Jesus Christ. The picture needed to represent the Savior so it needed to be done exactly as God commanded.

> **"Whatever has a defect, you shall not offer, for it will not be accepted for you. When a man offers a sacrifice of peace offerings to the Lord to fulfill a special vow or for a freewill offering, of the herd or of the flock, it must be perfect to be accepted; there shall be no defect in it. Those that are blind or fractured or maimed or having a running sore or eczema or scabs, you shall not offer to the Lord, nor make of them an offering by fire on the altar to the Lord. In respect to an ox or a lamb which has an overgrown or stunted member, you may present it for a freewill offering, but for a vow it will not be accepted."**
> (Leviticus 22:20-23)

> **"But if it has any defect, such as lameness or blindness, or any serious defect, you shall not sacrifice it to the Lord your God."**
> (Deuteronomy 15:21)

For anyone to offer a defective or second rate offering to God was not just disrespectful, but it was a defilement of His system. It was like saying the One pictured, the Lamb of God, is defiled or sinful.

The question posed back to the Jewish people who had been disrespectful was, "Would you invite the governor of the land over for dinner and put substandard food on the table?" Of course not! Then why would they even consider giving God anything less? The priests were the primary ones responsible since they were the ones given the responsibility to make sure the sacrifices and worship of the nation were honoring to God. They had been neglectful and even disgraceful in their duties. By intentionally offering sacrifices with physical defects (blind, lame, sick, etc.), they defiled the sacrificial system and defiled God.

God even said it would be better to "shut the doors," or stop all heartless, and useless worship rather than proceed in insincere worship. It is tiring to God to listen to hollow words and empty worship. This is not a new problem. Listen to Isaiah several centuries before:

> "'What are your multiplied sacrifices to Me?'
> Says the Lord.
> 'I have had enough of burnt offerings of rams
> And the fat of fed cattle;
> And I take no pleasure in the blood of bulls,
> lambs or goats.
> When you come to appear before Me,
> Who requires of you this trampling of My courts?
> "Bring your worthless offerings no longer,
> Incense is an abomination to Me.
> New moon and sabbath, the calling of assemblies—
> I cannot endure iniquity and the solemn assembly.
> "I hate your new moon festivals and your
> appointed feasts,
> They have become a burden to Me;
> I am weary of bearing them.
> "So when you spread out your hands in prayer,
> I will hide My eyes from you;
> Yes, even though you multiply prayers,
> I will not listen.
> Your hands are covered with blood.'"
> (Isaiah 1:11-15)

A funny story is told by pastors to illustrate the priority of giving God our best. A farmer once had a cow that was about to give birth and he prayed and told God that if the cow had two calves, he would give God one of them as a sacrificial gift. The cow did have two calves and the farmer reaffirmed his pledge. During the night one of the calves died. The next morning after discovering the dead calf he prayed to God, "Lord, I am sad to report to You that Your calf died last night!"

As humorous as this story may be, it is actually a picture of the condition of the people of God. They were not giving God their best but their leftovers. Let us never forget God is our King.

> **"'But cursed be the swindler who has a male in his flock and vows it, but sacrifices a blemished animal to the Lord, for I am a great King,' says the Lord of hosts, 'and My name is feared among the nations.'"** (1:14)

**APPLICATION** - Christian leaders today need to be very careful in the same way. Are we giving God our best? Are we faithful in studying God's Word so our people have proper feeding? Are we diligent to oversee the shepherding responsibility given to us by our Great Shepherd?

# Malachi 2
## Widespread sin in the land from the priests to the families.

### GOD REBUKED THE PRIESTS FOR THEIR MANY SINS (2:1-9)

¹ "And now this commandment is for you, O priests. ² If you do not listen, and if you do not take it to heart to give honor to My name," says the LORD OF HOSTS, "THEN I WILL SEND THE CURSE UPON YOU AND I WILL CURSE YOUR BLESSINGS; AND INDEED, I HAVE CURSED THEM *already*, because you are not taking *it* to heart. ³ Behold, I am going to rebuke your offspring, and I will spread refuse on your faces, the refuse of your feasts; and you will be taken away with it. ⁴ Then you will know that I have sent this commandment to you, that My covenant may continue with Levi," says the LORD OF HOSTS. ⁵ "My covenant with him was *one of* life and peace, and I gave them to him *as an object of* reverence; so he

revered Me and stood in awe of My name. [6] True instruction was in his mouth and unrighteousness was not found on his lips; he walked with Me in peace and uprightness, and he turned many back from iniquity. [7] For the lips of a priest should preserve knowledge, and men should seek instruction from his mouth; for he is the messenger of the LORD OF HOSTS. [8] But as for you, you have turned aside from the way; you have caused many to stumble by the instruction; you have corrupted the covenant of Levi," says the LORD OF HOSTS. [9] "So I also have made you despised and abased before all the people, just as you are not keeping My ways but are showing partiality in the instruction.

Even though God laid a strong guilty verdict on the priesthood of Israel in this section, He said He still wanted the priesthood to repent and return to their holy calling. He reminded them that from the beginning when He made a covenant with Levi in the time of Moses over 1,000 years earlier, He always wanted it to be a perpetual covenant. Read it again.

> "'Then you will know that I have sent this commandment to you, that My covenant may continue with Levi,' says the Lord of hosts. 'My covenant with him was one of life and peace, and I gave them to him as an object of reverence; so he revered Me and stood in awe of My name.'" (2:4, 5)

God did not want the priests to disqualify themselves, but to return to the holy dedication of Levi, the priestly line of Israel. That was the message to the priests, the spiritual leaders of the land. As we will see in the next section, the poor practices of the priest discouraged the people and they fell into the same meaningless worship practices. That is why God told them to just shut the doors of the temple. If the heart is not in it, then why just go through the motions, it is not real.

**APPLICATION** - Have you ever been in a church where the pastor, an elder or a deacon fell into sin? It soon became a public shame and discouraged the flock. If the strongest of the fellowship can't keep from sin then what hope does anyone have? Churches whose pastors fall or whose marriages fail often experience a landslide of sin in the congregation. People give up hope. That is why God puts responsibility on leaders.

> **"Let not many of you become teachers, my brethren, knowing that as such we will incur a stricter judgment."** (James 3:10)

It is hard to imagine a much harsher condemnation or description of what God thinks of the sins of the leadership than what He says in verse three:

> **"Behold, I am going to rebuke your offspring, and I will spread refuse on your faces, the refuse of your feasts; and you will be taken away with it."** (2:3)

In case there is any question of the meaning of refuse, the Greek concordance defines it's one and only meaning as "fecal matter, dung."

> **"This very graphic language shows how God viewed unfaithful priests as worthy of the most unthinkable disgrace. As the internal waste of the sacrificial animal was normally carried outside the camp and burned (cf.** Exodus 29:14; Leviticus 4:11, 12; 8:17; 16:27**), so the priests would be discarded and suffer humiliation and loss of office. The Lord's purpose in such a warning was to shake them out of their complacency."** (MacArthur Study Bible)

God still wanted His people to be in a covenant relationship and we know that He will always have a remnant faithful to Him. The door is always open for national repentance. If Christian leaders don't clean up their act, well, we heard what He will do.

## GOD REBUKED THE SINS OF THE FAMILIES OF ISRAEL (2:10-17)

[10] "Do we not all have one father? Has not one God created us? Why do we deal treacherously each against his brother so as to profane the covenant of our fathers? [11] Judah has dealt treacherously, and an abomination has been committed in Israel and in Jerusalem; for Judah has profaned the sanctuary of the LORD WHICH HE LOVES AND HAS MARRIED THE DAUGHTER OF A FOREIGN GOD. [12] *As* for the man who does this, may the LORD CUT OFF FROM THE TENTS OF JACOB *everyone* who awakes and answers, or who presents an offering to the LORD OF HOSTS.

[13] "This is another thing you do: you cover the altar of the LORD WITH TEARS, WITH WEEPING AND WITH GROANING, BECAUSE HE NO LONGER REGARDS THE OFFERING OR ACCEPTS *it with* favor from your hand. [14] Yet you say, 'For what reason?' Because the LORD HAS BEEN A WITNESS BETWEEN YOU AND THE WIFE OF YOUR YOUTH, AGAINST WHOM YOU HAVE DEALT TREACHEROUSLY, THOUGH SHE IS YOUR COMPANION AND YOUR WIFE BY COVENANT. [15] But not one has done *so* who has a remnant of the Spirit. And what did *that* one *do* while he was seeking a godly offspring? Take heed then to your spirit, and let no one deal treacherously against the wife of your youth. [16] For I hate divorce," says the LORD, THE GOD OF ISRAEL, "AND HIM WHO COVERS HIS GARMENT WITH WRONG," SAYS THE LORD OF HOSTS. "SO TAKE HEED TO YOUR SPIRIT, THAT YOU DO NOT DEAL TREACHEROUSLY." [17] You have wearied the LORD WITH YOUR WORDS. YET YOU SAY, "HOW HAVE WE WEARIED *Him*?" In that you say, "Everyone who does evil is good in the sight of the LORD, AND HE DELIGHTS IN THEM," OR, "WHERE IS THE GOD OF JUSTICE?"

Malachi moved on to the results of failed spiritual leadership. It produced failed family life and sinful practices in the congregation. The people embraced immoral practices, families fell apart in divorce and the men took wives from pagan nations. These prohibited practices were condemned by Ezra and Nehemiah 100 years before. There was even a great revival and putting away foreign wives. Times have changed again. Some fell back into that sinful pattern. God reminded the people *"let no one deal treacherously against the wife of your youth. For I hate divorce (2:15, 16)."*

The practice of marrying pagan women always brought disaster. Solomon's kingdom crumbled because his heart went after the gods his many wives brought into the palace. In Malachi's time, the same quicksand of sin was back again. It was easy to step in but getting out was not only difficult but sometimes next to impossible. An philosopher wrote, "The deceptive curse of sinful deed is that of new sin, it becomes the seed." Sin keeps reproducing. Like a gangrene infection in the body, it must be cut away and there is always loss.

God told the people that those who married foreign women must be cut off from the people. They have had ample warnings. The dying flesh of the body must be cut off.

> **"for Judah has profaned the sanctuary of the LORD WHICH HE LOVES AND HAS MARRIED THE DAUGHTER OF A FOREIGN GOD. As for the man who does this, may the LORD CUT OFF FROM THE TENTS OF JACOB"** (VERSES 11, 12)

The next question and answer sequence is introduced in this section.

> **"You have wearied the LORD WITH YOUR WORDS. YET YOU SAY, 'HOW HAVE WE WEARIED Him?' In that you say, 'Everyone who does evil is good in the sight of the LORD, AND HE DELIGHTS IN THEM,' OR, 'WHERE IS THE GOD OF JUSTICE?'"** (2:17)

For hundreds of years, God sent prophets over and over rebuking the people's empty religion and hollow practices. Yet, over and over again, they kept returning to their old sinful ways. Not only had they repeated the same failures of their fathers but had sunk to a new low. They were actually calling evil good. They were saying that to do evil was good in the sight of the Lord. God, they say, even delighted in the evil they did. How could a man fall that low to actually believe that? They actually blamed God because He had not brought justice to their enemies. Chapter one of Romans (400 years later) described the very same sins which even today plague the human race:

> "and although they know the ordinance of God, that those who practice such things are worthy of death, they not only do the same, but also give hearty approval to those who practice them." (Romans 1:32)

In review, we read that the spiritual condition of the priests had collapsed. That led to the ruin of many families when fathers left their wives and families to pursue false gods. The men that did this knew they had made a covenant with their wives and chose to break that covenant.

> "Because the Lord has been a witness between you and the wife of your youth, against whom you have dealt treacherously, though she is your companion and your wife by covenant." (2:14)

The very people who had abandoned their covenants with their wives were asking if God loved them. They wanted assurance that their sin did not nullify the covenant of God. They wanted to be safe but to still keep sinning. It is clear that it doesn't work that way. The misery of hypocritical faith is seen in verse 13:

> "This is another thing you do: you cover the altar of the Lord with tears, with weeping and with groaning, because

**He no longer regards the offering or accepts it with favor from your hand."** (2:13)

So, what was God going to do?  The next chapter will begin with the priests.

# Malachi 3
## A day is coming when Levi will again be a holy people

### TWO MESSENGERS ARE COMING (3:1)

¹ "Behold, I am going to send My messenger, and he will clear the way before Me. And the Lord, whom you seek, will suddenly come to His temple; and the Messenger of the covenant, in whom you delight, behold, He is coming," says the Lord of hosts.

The story of the Levites, the priestly tribe of Israel, is like a roller coaster, up and down, up and down. This prophecy of Malachi looks to the day when a great final cleansing will come. The sins of the priests will go through the purifying furnace of God. The two messengers Malachi describes will be the beginning of that cleansing which is described in the next few verses.

This is the final Messianic prophecy in the Old Testament. It describes what will happen when Christ is introduced to the world by John the Baptist. We need to understand what we can about the two messengers in this verse. The first messenger is sent to clear the way for the Lord. The second is described as coming to His temple as the Messenger of the Covenant. There seems to be little doubt that Jesus the Messiah is the One being announced by the first messenger. That first messenger is John the Baptist (Matthew 11:10, Mark 1:2, and Luke 7:27). Here is how the Message, a Bible paraphrase, translates Malachi 3:1:

> "Look! I'm sending my messenger on ahead to clear the way for me. Suddenly, out of the blue, the Leader you've been looking for will enter his Temple—yes, the Messenger of the Covenant, the one you've been waiting for. Look! He's on his way!" A Message from the mouth of God-of-the-Angel-Armies." (The Message)

Even though this verse describes two distinct messengers, the same Greek word (*Malik*) is used for both. This can be confusing. The following is the Greek usage:

> ### *04397 mal'ak*
>
> *from an unused root meaning to dispatch as a deputy...*
>
> *AV - angel 111, messenger 98, ambassadors 4, variant 1; 214*
>
> 1) *messenger, representative*
>    1a) *messenger*
>    1b) *angel*
>    1c) *the theophanic angel (Can refer to an epiphany, a message from on high, usually an angel, or it could be a theophany, which is an actual appearance of God Himself)*

The Greek word has a wide range of meanings. It could describe an angel, a person bringing a message or an actual appearance of God in our world.

John the Baptist is the first '*Malak*', 'messenger', of Malachi 3:1: *"'Behold, I send My messenger ['Malak'], and he will prepare the way before Me."* Jesus identifies him *"For this is he of whom it is written: 'Behold, I send My messenger before Your face, Who will prepare Your way before You.' Assuredly, I say to you, among those born of women there has not risen one greater than John the Baptist; but he who is least in the kingdom of heaven is greater than he."* (Matthew 11:10-11).

The second 'Malak', the 'Messenger of the Covenant,' is the ultimate theophany, God Himself, God incarnate, Jesus Christ.

Malachi refers to a Messianic prophecy first spoken in Isaiah 40:3

> **The voice of one crying in the wilderness:**
> **"Prepare the way of the LORD;**
> **Make straight in the desert**
> **A highway for our God.** (Isaiah 40:3)

Remember, this is the last word from God before He closes the pages of the Old Testament. The next time the people will hear from God will be from the two messengers in this prophecy, John the Baptist and the Lord Jesus Christ. The very last words of chapter four, as we will see, is that the first messenger coming will come in power like Elijah. He will be the one crying in the wilderness that The Lamb of God has come to take away the sins of the world. We will talk more about that in Malachi four.

## WHAT THE MESSIAH WILL DO WHEN HE COMES. (3:2-6)

² "But who can endure the day of His coming? And who can stand when He appears? For He is like a refiner's fire and like fullers' soap. ³ He will sit as a smelter and purifier of silver, and He will purify the sons of Levi and refine them like gold and silver, so that they may present to the LORD OFFERINGS IN RIGHTEOUSNESS. ⁴ Then the offering of Judah and Jerusalem will be pleasing to the LORD AS IN THE DAYS OF OLD AND AS IN FORMER YEARS.

⁵ "Then I will draw near to you for judgment; and I will be a swift witness against the sorcerers and against the adulterers and against those who swear falsely, and against those who oppress the wage earner in his wages, the widow and the orphan, and those who turn aside the alien and do not fear Me," says the LORD OF HOSTS. ⁶ "For I, the LORD, DO NOT CHANGE; THEREFORE YOU, O SONS OF JACOB, ARE NOT CONSUMED.

He is coming! In Matthew 4:6 we read, *"The people who live in darkness have seen a great light, and for those living in the shadowland of death, light has dawned."*

If God were described as the brightest light, sin would be the darkest night. Nothing about sin is compatible with God. When Jesus became our sin on the cross (2 Corinthians 5:21), The Father turned His eyes away from His Son. This passage is about God dealing with His sinful priests. That is why it begins with the question, *"But who can endure the day of His coming? And who can stand when He appears?"* If we ever question just how repulsive sin is to God, remember that the Last Judgment will send all who have died in their sin to an eternal banishment into the Lake of Fire. It helps to review what happens when God shows up for the final justice against sin.

> **"Then I saw a great white throne and Him who sat upon it, from whose presence earth and heaven fled away, and no place was found for them."** (Revelation 20:11)

The entire universe was created by God and is currently cursed because of the fall (Romans eight). It will have to be replaced by a New Heaven and Earth with no more curse. If the current universe flees from the presence of God, trying to hide from His Glory and holiness, then *"who can endure the day of His coming? And who can stand when He appears?"* (3.2)

For the sons of Levi, the priests, the coming of Jesus will be like a great smelting furnace where the precious metals are purified. All sin, dross, and impurities will be melted away. *"He is like a refiner's fire." "He will purify the sons of Levi, and purge them as gold and silver."* John the Baptist, the first messenger introduced Jesus to the priests and crowd:

> **"As for me, I baptize you with water; but One is coming who is mightier than I, and I am not fit to untie the thong of His sandals; He will baptize you with the Holy Spirit and fire. His winnowing fork is in His hand to thoroughly clear His threshing floor, and to gather the wheat into His barn; but He will burn up the chaff with unquenchable fire."** (Matthew 3:11, 12)

One of the tests of a purified metal is that the refiner will know the metal is pure when he can see his own reflection in the metal. God is making us into the image of His Son but it is a violent process at times. So much has to be taken out but *"When He has tried me, I shall come forth as gold"* (Job 23:10).

> **"All discipline for the moment seems not to be joyful, but sorrowful; yet to those who have been trained by it, afterward, it yields the peaceful fruit of righteousness."** (Hebrews 12:11).

The illustration of the soap makers' soap is also given.

> **"Purify me from my sins, and I will be clean;**
> **wash me, and I will be whiter than snow."** (Psalm 51:7)

Both the smelting furnace and cleaning by soap are describing the cleansing from sin for the sons of Levi. *"Who shall ascend into the hill of the Lord? or who shall stand in his holy place? He that hath clean hands, and a pure heart" (Psalm 24:3,4).* Then their offerings will be accepted by God.

**"That they may offer to the LORD  
An offering in righteousness.  
Then the offering of Judah and Jerusalem  
Will be pleasant to the LORD"** *(3:4)*

Many believe that this is a double prophecy about Christ's first and second coming. Albert Barnes and others say:

> **"Malachi seems to blend, as Joel, the first and second coming of our Lord. It is then one ever-present judgment."**

When Jesus walked the earth, He came as the Savior from sin, but also a fire of judgment against the false shepherds who had led the people of God astray. The Gospel offered hope to the sinner and cleansing from sin but also resulted in a judgement for all who rejected God's Messenger, the Messiah. This message is just as real today as in the time of Christ. It is one "ever-present judgment."

Judgment always begins with the house of God. Following the purification of the priests of Levi, God then turned His attention to the people. He began with the false teachers and the sorcerers and then the adulterous sins in the land (3:5). Many sins of the people are listed: sorcery, adultery, perjury, exploitation of fellow man, mistreating orphans and widows and refusing to help outsiders. Their sins had cut them off from the very people they were supposed to help. The nation was to be a lighthouse to the nations and they didn't even help their own struggling people.

When the Great Messenger (Jesus) came He went to both the priestly class and Pharisees and to the multitudes. He preached the Kingdom of God. His message was very different from what the teachers of the Law had been telling them. They were blind teachers leading their blind followers into the ditch.

The root issue of all this is given at the end of verse five:

> **"Because they do not fear Me,**
> **Says the LORD of hosts."** (3:5)

God reminded them that if they would only come home, He would be there waiting for them. His promises are always true. The only reason the children of Israel were not treated like the godless nations is that God has remained faithful to His promises and covenants.

> **"For I, the LORD, DO NOT CHANGE; THEREFORE YOU, O SONS OF JACOB, ARE NOT CONSUMED."** (3:6)

The invitation has always been there. Just come home to your Father.

## THE PEOPLE THAT FORGOT HOW TO GET HOME (3:7)

7 "From the days of your fathers you have turned aside from My statutes and have not kept *them*. Return to Me, and I will return to you," says the LORD OF HOSTS. "BUT YOU SAY, 'HOW SHALL WE RETURN?'

One of the sad things that sometimes happens to older people is they can become disoriented. Friends or family have to search for the one who went somewhere and did not return. The person will usually be confused, not remembering how to get home. Israel became like that. The priesthood was corrupted for generations so the message of repentance and forgiveness was clouded. They were sheep without a shepherd. Over the years of living in a backslidden condition, they had forgotten that there was a way home.

In the next verses we will find that there was a first step they needed to take to get back on the path home.

## ROBBING GOD (3:8-12)

[8] "Will a man rob God? Yet you are robbing Me! But you say, 'How have we robbed You?' In tithes and offerings. [9] You are cursed with a curse, for you are robbing Me, the whole nation *of you*! [10] Bring the whole tithe into the storehouse, so that there may be food in My house, and test Me now in this," says the LORD OF HOSTS, "IF I WILL NOT OPEN FOR YOU THE WINDOWS OF HEAVEN AND POUR OUT FOR YOU A BLESSING UNTIL IT OVERFLOWS. [11] Then I will rebuke the devourer for you, so that it will not destroy the fruits of the ground; nor will your vine in the field cast *its grapes*," says the LORD OF HOSTS. [12] "All the nations will call you blessed, for you shall be a delightful land," says the LORD OF HOSTS.

Many people in the churches today are not familiar with the minor prophets. Malachi 3:8-10 is one of the few passages they have been taught. Most likely many are tired of hearing their pastors use it to try to increase giving.

In the previous verses, the people asked how they could return to God and get in the right relationship again. These verses are a natural solution to the problem. Where a person puts his treasure, that is where his heart can be found (Matthew 6:21). God told them in the previous verse that the heart of the people was far from Him. So, how do the people get their hearts back to God?

A natural starting place is to get back to the tithing commands of God. The book of Haggai a century before described the same problem. The Temple needed to be rebuilt but the people decided their own comfort needs were more important than the plan of God. They stopped building the Temple and began working on their own houses instead, even using materials designated for the Temple to panel their homes. God sent a drought upon them and the entire nation suffered. Fortunately, they listened to Haggai and repented. They completed the Temple. They put their time, talent and treasure to work for God instead of their own self-interests.

Malachi was calling the people to do the same. God condemned the people because they had robbed Him. How? By not tithing, not giving at least 10% of their income to the Lord. The word "tithe" means "a tenth." Actually, when the Jews followed all that God had instructed, the amount was much higher than 10%. The people in Malachi's time were not giving the bare minimum. Their heart was not with God since their treasure was not given to God.

Most of the tithe was given in the form of grain. These were farming people and the grain was stored in storehouses. The food was used for various things but one of the needs was to help provide for the Levites and priests. They were the only tribe that did not have land and so they could not grow their own food.

> **"You shall not forsake the Levite who is within your gates, for he has no part nor inheritance with you. At the end of every third year you shall bring out the tithe of your produce of that year and store it up within your gates. And the Levite, because he has no portion nor inheritance with you, and the stranger and the fatherless and the widow who are within your gates, may come and eat and be satisfied, that the LORD your God may bless you in all the work of your hand which you do."**
> (Deuteronomy 14:27-29)

The priests handled the sacrifices. The way of salvation by faith was presented by them. It was all an important picture of the Lamb of God who would be sacrificed for our sins. The tithe was an important provision to keep the message of salvation available to all the people. By robbing God, the people were robbing their own people by starving the ones who brought the hope of forgiveness to the nation. The very system that showed man how to return to God was not being supported so the people did not know how to return to God.

That was the point of what Malachi was trying to show them. They had just heard that God wanted them to return to Him and they said they didn't know how. Malachi in chapter three was telling them how. Start by tithing again. God wants to bless you. He will open the windows of heaven for you if you will just take this simple step of faith and support His Old Testament Gospel program.

Finally, God promised to stop the famine that devoured the crops. He promised to make Israel a blessing to the nations. They will be called the *"delightful land."*

## THE BLINDNESS OF PRIDE (3:13-15)

[13] "Your words have been arrogant against Me," says the LORD. "YET YOU SAY, 'WHAT HAVE WE SPOKEN AGAINST YOU?' [14] You have said, 'It is vain to serve God; and what profit is it that we have kept His charge, and that we have walked in mourning before the LORD OF HOSTS? [15] So now we call the arrogant blessed; not only are the doers of wickedness built up but they also test God and escape.'"

God, as prosecuting attorney, continued His charges. He told the people that they had arrogantly been resisting Him. Once again, they challenged His charges, *"What have we spoken against You?"* God explained His charges against them.

The people claimed it was *"vain"*, or useless, to serve God. The reason they gave was the prosperity of the wicked. Those who did not follow God were doing well. They didn't give up their grain to feed the priests and the poor. They mocked and tested God but they didn't suffer the consequences like the people of

God. They were saying, "They were prospering but we aren't."

The story is told of two farmers, one a Christian and the other an atheist. The atheist laughed at the Christian that he did not plant or harvest on the Lord's day, losing a valuable amount of time to produce a strong crop. When the Fall season came, the time for harvest, the atheist had a larger crop and ridiculed the Christian that he now had more money. The Christian simply said, "God doesn't balance His books in November."

The Jews were saying when we tithe, we have less and are not as successful as those who refuse to follow God. What is the point of doing what God commands if it only hurts us? Asaph in Psalm 73 said the very same thing but then he realized something important that needed to be kept in mind:

> **"Surely God is good to Israel,**
> **To those who are pure in heart!**
> **But as for me, my feet came close to stumbling,**
> **My steps had almost slipped.**
> **For I was envious of the arrogant**
> **As I saw the prosperity of the wicked.**
> **For there are no pains in their death,**
> **And their body is fat."** (Psalm 73:1-4)

But then Asaph saw that there was more to the story than temporary prosperity.

> **"When I pondered to understand this,**
> **It was troublesome in my sight**
> **Until I came into the sanctuary of God;**
> **Then I perceived their end.**
> **Surely You set them in slippery places;**
> **You cast them down to destruction."**
> (Psalm 73:16-18)

> **"Whom have I in heaven but You?**
> **And besides You, I desire nothing on earth.**
> **My flesh and my heart may fail,**

But God is the strength of my heart and my portion
forever. For, behold, those who are far from You will
perish;
You have destroyed all those who are unfaithful to You.
But as for me, the nearness of God is my good;
I have made the Lord God my refuge, That I may tell of all
Your works." (Psalm 73:25-28)

The Jews were only looking at the short picture, the temporary, the temporal things, but had lost sight of the eternal things. This is a relevant lesson today just as it was in Malachi's time. The apostle Paul had to remind the Corinthian Church just as Malachi had to remind his people:

"Therefore we do not lose heart, but though our outer
man is decaying, yet our inner man is being renewed day
by day. For momentary, light affliction is producing for
us an eternal weight of glory far beyond all comparison,
while we look not at the things which are seen, but at the
things which are not seen; for the things which are seen
are temporal, but the things which are not seen are
eternal." (2 Corinthians 4:16-18)

## THE BOOK OF REMEMBRANCE (3:16-18)

[16] Then those who feared the LORD SPOKE TO ONE ANOTHER, AND THE LORD GAVE ATTENTION AND HEARD *it*, and a book of remembrance was written before Him for those who fear the LORD AND WHO ESTEEM HIS NAME. [17] "They will be Mine," says the LORD OF HOSTS, "ON THE DAY THAT I PREPARE *My* own possession, and I will spare them as a man spares his own son who serves him." [18] So you will again distinguish between the righteous and the wicked, between one who serves God and one who does not serve Him.

**What is the book of remembrance Malachi describes?**

We had previously seen that the people felt it was useless to
serve God since those who did not serve God were not

punished. They got away with their selfish behavior. Israel wondered if God even cared if they obeyed or not. Did God even notice them? The answer is given in these verses. God was definitely noticing and He was recording it all in a "*Book of Remembrance*." The following quotation from the **Got Questions** website is an excellent explanation.

> "The book of Malachi is a detailed account from the Lord to Israel about their disobedience. His charges against them include offering defective sacrifices (1:8), teaching error (2:8), being unfaithful to their wives (2:13–14), and complaining that it was futile to serve the Lord (3:13–14). God pronounces strict judgments upon those guilty of such offenses (Malachi 2:2, 9). He then makes it clear that He hears and knows the intent of every heart and desires to honor those who honor Him. He knows those who refuse to murmur against Him (Numbers 14:27, 36; Deuteronomy 1:27; Psalm 106:25).
>
> Several places in Scripture refer to God's "book" (Exodus 32:32; Psalm 56:8; 69:28; Daniel 7:10; 12:1; Revelation 13:8; 20:15). In His infinite knowledge, God does not need a written record in order to keep track of human deeds. However, when He speaks to us, He often uses metaphor or parable to help us understand (see Mark 4:33). As Malachi presented God's words to the people, they would have understood what a book of remembrance represented. The kings of Persia kept such books, records of those who had rendered service to the king, that those servants might be rewarded. The book of Esther contains a good example of this (Esther 6:1–3).
>
> It is also important to note that the reward was often delayed. That's why books were needed, so that no worthy deed for the king went unrewarded. In Malachi 3:17 the Lord says, "'On the day when I act . . . .'" He is indicating that faithful service may go on for years with no apparent reward, but He is taking note. There is coming a day when He will act. One reason the Israelites had grown lax in their obedience and were becoming

jealous of evildoers was that they thought the Lord did not see or care (Malachi 3:14–15; cf. Psalm 94:7; Ezekiel 8:12).

However, Scripture is clear that loyalty to God does not go unnoticed or unrewarded. Jesus spoke of this many times (Matthew 10:42; Mark 9:41; Luke 6:23; Revelation 22:12). He spoke of storing up treasure in heaven, as though making deposits into a bank account (Matthew 6:20). The implication is that what is done on earth is forever recorded in heaven (2 Corinthians 5:10). The book of remembrance is simply a concept God used to encourage His faithful ones that their love and service for Him was appreciated. It is His promise that, when His judgment comes against those who reject Him, He knows His own and will preserve them.

The account of righteous Noah is a good illustration of God preserving those who honor Him (Genesis 6:9). Jesus encouraged His followers to "rejoice that your names are written in heaven" (Luke 10:20). Even as He said it, Jesus knew that their faithfulness to Him would result in earthy trouble, heartache, and even death (Matthew 24:9; Acts 9:16; 12:2). But knowing that their names were written in God's book helped the disciples persevere to the end (Matthew 10:22; Mark 13:13).

Galatians 6:9 continues the theme of future reward: "Let us not grow weary of doing good, for in due season we will reap, if we do not give up." Those who continue to honor the Lord when many around them fall away can rest in the confidence that their names are written in God's book of remembrance." (Got Questions website)

The purpose of these final verses in Malachi three was to encourage the faithful that God does notice and has a special book with their names recorded. He tells them they are His and He prepares them as a special possession. The Hebrew word translated "possession" means a special treasure, like a crown of brilliant jewels. That is how God sees His children. We are His special prized treasure, shining jewels reflecting His glory. That alone should be enough to keep our eyes off the temporary pleasures and fading victories of the lost world. It isn't so much that they have things we don't, but we have what they don't. Remember, those who don't know God also have a "*book of remembrance*" which will be opened at the last judgment.

> **"Then I saw a great white throne and Him who sat upon it, from whose presence earth and heaven fled away, and no place was found for them. And I saw the dead, the great and the small, standing before the throne, and books were opened; and another book was opened, which is the book of life; and the dead were judged from the things which were written in the books, according to their deeds. And the sea gave up the dead which were in it, and death and Hades gave up the dead which were in them; and they were judged, every one of them according to their deeds. Then death and Hades were thrown into the lake of fire. This is the second death, the lake of fire. And if anyone's name was not found written in the book of life, he was thrown into the lake of fire."**

(Revelation 20:11-15)

# Malachi 4

## THE AWESOME DAY OF THE LORD IS COMING (4:1-3)

[1] "For behold, the day is coming, burning like a furnace; and all the arrogant and every evildoer will be chaff; and the day that is coming will set them ablaze," says the Lord of hosts, "so that it will leave them neither root nor branch." [2] "But for you who fear My name, the sun of righteousness will rise with healing in its wings; and you will go forth and skip about like calves from the stall. [3] You will tread down the wicked, for they will be ashes under the soles of your feet on the day which I am preparing," says the Lord of hosts.

Malachi referred to this coming Messiah as the "Sun of Righteousness." The early church writers identified this phrase as describing Jesus. The brilliant glory of God was veiled in human flesh. John said, *"And the Word was made flesh and dwelt among us, and we beheld his glory, the glory as of the only begotten of the Father, full of grace and truth."* (John 1:14).

> **"The people that walked in darkness have seen a great light: they that dwell in the land of the shadow of death, upon them hath the light shined."** (Isaiah 9:2)

The book of Revelation describes Jesus as He appeared to John in His glory.

> **"I saw one like a son of man, clothed in a robe reaching to the feet, and girded across His chest with a golden sash. His head and His hair were white like white wool, like**

snow; and His eyes were like a flame of fire. His feet were like burnished bronze, when it has been made to glow in a furnace, and His voice was like the sound of many waters. In His right hand He held seven stars, and out of His mouth came a sharp two-edged sword; and His face was like the sun shining in its strength."

(Revelation 1:14-16)

The Messiah, Jesus, in His glory is called the "sun of Righteousness" to His chosen people. When Jesus rose from the dead He came forth in power and glory to restore His children. The lost will have a different encounter. They will encounter the scorching judgment of His holiness and be set ablaze like the chaff from the wheat fields in a great fire. The believers will be like joyful newborn calves released from the pen to run through the pasture. The evildoers will be ash under the feet of the people of the Kingdom of God. They will have no hope in eternity, and will never rise out of the ashes. We are told they have no root or branch, nothing left that has the hope of life again. It is a very sobering description of the destiny of the redeemed and the destiny of the lost.

## THE DAYS OF ELIJAH – THE LAST PROPHECY IN THE OLD TESTAMENT (4:4-6)

⁴ "Remember the law of Moses My servant, *even the* statutes and ordinances which I commanded him in Horeb for all Israel. ⁵ "Behold, I am going to send you Elijah the prophet before the coming of the great and terrible day of the LORD. ⁶ He will restore the hearts of the fathers to *their* children and the hearts of the children to their fathers, so that I will not come and smite the land with a curse."

Malachi closed the Old Testament and all written prophecy for 400 years. The silence would eventually be broken by the one who came in the spirit and power of Elijah. That one was the forerunner of Christ. He was *"a voice crying in the wilderness,"* John the Baptist. He, as we know today, announced the Messiah, Jesus, to the world. The final prophecy in the Old Testament is that Elijah the prophet is coming back. His work was apparently not finished. He went to heaven in a whirlwind and never saw death (2 Kings 2:11). Some think God must have had another assignment for him in the future.

There are two New Testament Scriptures that need to be looked at concerning this prophecy. The first is in Luke when the birth of John the Baptist is announced to Elizabeth and Zacharias. Malachi four is quoted as applying to John the Baptist:

> **"But the angel said to him, 'Do not be afraid, Zacharias, for your petition has been heard, and your wife Elizabeth will bear you a son, and you will give him the name John. You will have joy and gladness, and many will rejoice at his birth. For he will be great in the sight of the Lord; and he will drink no wine or liquor, and he will be filled with the Holy Spirit while yet in his mother's womb. And he will turn many of the sons of Israel back to the Lord their God. It is he who will go as a forerunner before Him in the spirit and power of Elijah, to turn the hearts of the fathers back to the children, and the disobedient to the attitude of the righteous, so as to make ready a people prepared for the Lord.'"** (Luke 1:13-17)

The second passage is in Matthew. Jesus is talking about Elijah and John the Baptist.

> **"Truly I say to you, among those born of women there has not arisen anyone greater than John the Baptist! Yet the one who is least in the kingdom of heaven is greater than he. From the days of John the Baptist until now the kingdom of heaven suffers violence, and violent men take it by force. For all the prophets and the Law prophesied until John. And if you are willing to accept it, John himself is Elijah who was to come. He who has ears to hear, let him hear."** (Matthew 11:11-15)

The first thing we can be sure of is that Malachi's prophecy was fulfilled either in part or in full in John the Baptist. The use of the term *"before the coming of the great and terrible day of the Lord"* (4:5) would normally refer to the time of the second coming of Jesus. Is it the first coming or the second coming? The Luke passage quotes only part of Malachi's prophecy. He did not mention the great and terrible day of the Lord. The following is how one theologian explains it.

> **"This was fulfilled in John the Baptist in a figurative sense** (Matthew 11:14, Mark 9:11-13, Luke 1:17**). Yet because this Elijah comes before the coming of the great and dreadful day, we know that the Elijah prophecy is only completely fulfilled before the Second Coming of Jesus.** John 17:11-12 **and** Revelation 11:3-12 **speak of this future fulfillment, when God will either send Elijah back to the earth on this special errand or send someone uniquely empowered in the spirit and office of Elijah. (Guzik, Blue Letter Bible)"**

It was not uncommon for the prophets to give a single prophecy that contained different times of fulfillment. There is some mystery in this. Is John the Baptist the complete fulfillment of Malachi's prophecy or is there a dual fulfillment? It is probable that it is referring to both, the first coming and ultimately when Christ returns on the great and terrible day of the Lord. For now, the fine details are still hazy. One thing, however, is certain, God knows the final details and it will happen.

Some have suggested that from the prophets perspective they saw a mountain range and it looks like all the mountain peaks are together. But they are actually two separate ranges separated by a large valley between them. They just look like one mountain range. Did Malachi see such a mountain range that had the ministry of John the Baptist and the second coming in one composite picture?

The Jewish people today continue to celebrate the Passover each year. They, of course, are still looking for their Messiah. They still believe Elijah is yet to come to announce the Messiah. Every Passover meal in every Jewish home always has an empty chair for Elijah in case he shows up.

The last part of the passage is about families being reconciled, fathers and sons. It also says sons will be reconciled to the fathers which could indicate a  deeper reconciliation.

The wayward sons who have left the faith will not only come home to their earthly fathers but **will also** be reconciled to the faith itself and their Jewish fathers, Abraham, Isaac, and Jacob. One day all will finally recognize and bow the knee to "the sun of Righteousness," The King of kings Himself.

> **"Being found in appearance as a man, He humbled Himself by becoming obedient to the point of death, even death on a cross. For this reason also, God highly exalted Him, and bestowed on Him the name which is above every name, so that at the name of Jesus every knee will bow, of those who are in heaven and on earth and under the earth, and that _every tongue_ will confess that Jesus Christ is Lord, to the glory of God the Father."**
> (Philippians 2:8-11)

## Amen and Amen!